Albert J. Luxford,
the Gimmick Man

Dedicated to the wonderful casts, crews
and audiences that enabled me to do the job I loved
and, in particular, my dear departed friends
John Stears and Desmond Llewelyn.

Albert J. Luxford, the Gimmick Man

Memoir of a Special Effects Maestro

ALBERT J. LUXFORD
with GARETH OWEN

foreword by DESMOND "Q" LLEWELYN
afterword by JOHN RICHARDSON

McFarland & Company, Inc., Publishers
Jefferson, North Carolina, and London

ISBN 978-0-7864-1150-4 (softcover : 50# alkaline paper)

Library of Congress cataloguing data are available

British Library cataloguing data are available

Manufactured in the United States of America

Cover photographs (clockwise from upper left): Bert and
the BSA Lightning from *Thunderball*; Bert with the
model helicopter from *From Russia with Love*, and
the laser table scene from *Goldfinger*

McFarland & Company, Inc., Publishers
Box 611, Jefferson, North Carolina 28640
www.mcfarlandpub.com

Acknowledgments

Morris Bright, Desmond Llewelyn, Joan Luxford, Peter Manley, John Richardson, Audrey Skinner, Dave Worrall.

Particular thanks to Robin Harbour, and Graham Rye of The James Bond International Fan Club & Archive for supplying such wonderful photographs, and to Matt Clark and Andrew Boyle for burning them onto CD.

The James Bond International Fan Club & Archive
PO Box 007
Addlestone
Surrey
KT15 1DY

www.thejamesbondfanclub.com

Contents

Scene Fourteen: Breaking In
Words of advice for would-be effects technicians.

A Note to the Reader

Bert Luxford and I decided to write this book largely in the third person. We felt that in this way we could best keep up the narrative of a long and rich career while interspersing Bert's personal recollections and anecdotes directly as he remembered them, to keep it lively. We think the interplay of fact and color works well and hope you do too.

Gareth Owen

Foreword

by Desmond "Q" Llewelyn

Ever since I first appeared as Q in *From Russia with Love* back in 1963, audiences seem to await the character's (brief!) appearance with some anticipation. I'm sure it's not me alone that generates such excitement, but those marvelous gadgets that 007 is equipped with before he goes out into the field — gadgets that save his life on many occasions.

People seem somewhat surprised when they meet me to learn that, after nearly 40 years of playing Q, I am utterly useless with gadgets. They always go wrong for me, and I can rarely understand them — even the video recorder causes me headaches when I want to record a program. There seems to be this perception that between films I actually work in Q-Branch making new gadgets; that couldn't be further from the truth! In fact, it's a very talented team of special effects people that bring the things to life. And they're quite often ahead of their time too, as many of the older gadgets have proven to be prototypes for modern-day ones.

The early Bond films had a great many wonderful gadgets and gimmicks. Who could forget the marvelous briefcase, the underwater breathing device or the Aston Martin DB5? The man behind the majority of the gadgets in the early films was Bert Luxford. Working with a marvelous team, he took the ideas of production designer Ken Adam and turned them into very clever working mechanisms and prototypes.

Of course, I then had the job of demonstrating and explaining them

1

Bert Luxford (center), Desmond Llewelyn (right) and his biographer Sandy Hernu two weeks before Desmond's tragic car accident. Gareth Owen Collection.

to 007; some of the lines were a bit technical, to say the least. Thank goodness I now have an assistant in the films to learn all those sorts of lines!

The early Bond films certainly set the standard — and not just for future episodes, but for action films as a whole — and there really wasn't anything else like them; and as far as I'm concerned, the gadgets were a very big part of that.

December 1999

SCENE ONE

Pay Attention, 007!

The scene: Pinewood Film Studios, morning.
The scenario: Just another average day in the engineering workshop.
The characters: A. J. Luxford, F. Newbury, S. Cain
The story: A well-known art director (Syd Cain) came into the workshop and asked the governor, Fred Newbury, if he had anyone in the department who could build "this"—and he produced a sketch on a piece of paper.

Fred said, "I've only got one bloke in here who's capable of doing that sort of thing ... maybe he'll say he can do it, maybe not, but go and talk to Bert over there."

"We've never met," Syd Cain said, as he greeted Bert Luxford, "but I'd like you to do a job for me."

"Yes, sir?"

With that, Cain handed him the sketch—an attaché case with certain modifications and extras.

"How long have I got?" Bert asked.

"Oh, about six to eight weeks. Do you think you can do it?"

Bert looked at it, sized it all up and said that he could probably do it. With that, Syd chipped in rather nonchalantly, "I want two!"—as if he was buying packets of sweets.

"Two!" exclaimed Bert. "Well, I might need a little help on them."

The case had leather inner and outer coverings, but with union rules and regulations being what they were then, Bert, as an engineer,

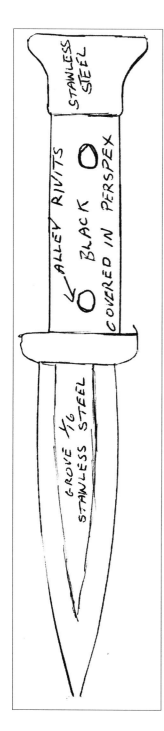

STAINLESS STEEL

ALLEY RIVITS

BLACK

COVERED IN PERSPEX

GROVE 1/16 STAINLESS STEEL

was not allowed to cover the cases with leather; that was the job of the upholstery department. It might sound a bit pedantic nowadays, but nobody was allowed to cross the line: Each person had a trade, and each stuck to it! The case was made in two separate sections — outer and inner — to accommodate the different gimmicks required (the knives, catches, sovereigns, etc.) which were not quite what they seemed, as Bert revealed, "In fact, the sovereigns were gold-sprayed shilling pieces! We couldn't afford the real things."

A month or so later, Bert completed his work and the aluminum cases were ready to go over to the upholsters who covered them in quality leather.

One was subsequently handed to Desmond Llewelyn for his first scene in his first Bond film, *From Russia with Love.*

Desmond, as the gadget-master Q, came into M's office with the case and explained the operation to Sean Connery's 007: Press here and out pops a throwing knife ... 20 gold sovereigns and a sniper's rifle inside and, observe how to open the case safely — turn the openers 90 degrees or the tear gas canister will go off ...

It was all good stuff and the first real Q-Branch gadget ever used in the Bond films.

The gadgets became a trademark of the films and Desmond's appearance was eagerly anticipated in each new Bond adventure. Q is very much a character "the back room boys" identify with as he so epitomizes them, and their work. They, just as Q, fully realize that months of hard toil are so often abused and destroyed by the operatives — be it 007, or just Johnny film director.

It would be untrue to suggest that Ian Fleming based his "Quartermaster" on Bert Luxford, as it was in fact Charles Fraser-Smith who inspired

Opposite: The attaché case knife design used in *From Russia with Love.*

the character, but Bert was the man responsible for bringing the marvelous, and some say futuristic, gadgets to life.

It wasn't strictly my first assignment for Commander Bond, but more on that later; however, it was certainly the one that set the standard for the gadgets that followed, and presented me with a real challenge. In fact, it lead to me being dubbed "The Gimmick Man."

SCENE TWO

The Beginnings

What exactly are "special effects"? They play an increasingly important part in film making, have Oscars bestowed upon their technicians, and yet are a bit of a mystery to the average film goer.

There are many types of effects (physical, visual, computer-generated), yet all the very different methods combine to one common result: convincing the audience that what they are seeing is real and really happening. Some effects are very expensive and involve a lot of people and machines whereas others are inexpensive, simple and achieved without masses of manpower or machine power. There is no real rule of thumb.

Special effects are, in essence, processes whereby illusions are created. Be it an actor falling down a bottomless pit, a car driving through a wall of flames or windows shattering under an explosion, all require an effects man to ensure the sequences are achieved safely, successfully and realistically. If you notice the effects, then the technician hasn't done his (or her) job properly. Perhaps that is partly the reason for the effects man remaining pretty much in the shadows, as far as film watchers are concerned. Just like a great illusionist, he keeps an air of mystery about him, for his secrets and tricks of the trade are mastered only after serving a long and hard apprenticeship in the front line of film making.

Just as the twentieth century witnessed the birth of film as we know it, it also served to nurture technology in the medium. What can be achieved nowadays is nothing short of staggering.

The special effects business in Britain was still in its relative infancy in the 1950s. There were no training or college courses, and there was little literature concerning the profession. However, a select few of the leading film and effects technicians soon revolutionized the business with their incredible foresight, ability and imagination. One of these few, in the British film industry, was Albert J. Luxford.

The First Job and Will Hay

Having left school at 16, Bert Luxford was secured a position, through his father, at the Institute of Automobile Engineers in West London. It wasn't exactly the career young Bert had his heart set on, as he dearly wanted to enter the medical profession. But practicalities prevailed — the family was comfortable but by no means wealthy enough to support a son through medical school.

Bert threw himself into his apprenticeship, although he wasn't called an apprentice — rather a "trainee technical assistant," specializing in engines.

> There I was, for quite a long time, involved in the Rolls Royce Merlin aircraft engine development — not the whole thing, but certain aspects of it, which I found to be absolutely fascinating and it gave me a solid grounding in the engineering trade.

The Institute held an annual open day when high profile figures in both engineering and public life would visit, but not before the trainees had polished and painted everything! Bert recalls, "If it doesn't move, paint it, they used to say."

Much to Bert's delight, one of the people he met on his first open day was British comedy actor Will Hay.

Born in 1888, Will Hay was probably one of Britain's most versatile entertainers. In addition to being a first-class comedian, he was also a distinguished astronomer (he discovered the spot on Saturn in 1933), a fully qualified pilot and formerly an engineer himself.

In 1922, Hay was launched into radio with comedy sketches of "St. Michaels School" where he played the headmaster. The popularity of the character was such that he transferred to film in the early 1930s. He worked at Elstree, then Gainsborough and, finally, Ealing Studios. His most successful period was almost definitely the Gainsborough years where he teamed up with director Marcel Varnel, writers Val Guest and Marriott Edgar, and the supporting cast duo of Moore Marriott and Graham Moffatt. Their films together included *Old Bones of the River, Windbag the*

Sailor, *Ask a Policeman*, *Convict 99* and the brilliant *Oh Mr. Porter*. Hay often co-wrote many of his films as well as taking a hand in the direction and was quite simply a genius of early British comedy cinema. He died in his mid-fifties—almost ten years after starring in his first film and finding "fame."

> Will Hay was a joy to meet, and I'm so proud to say that I had that opportunity. I grew up visiting the cinema two or three times a week as a child, and had seen his films many times over — he was a big box office star. I still watch them on video now! So you can appreciate just how exciting it was for me, but even more exciting was the fact that, having shaken hands with him, he explained he had been an engineer himself, and so he took great interest in what we were doing and had a lovely talk with me. I wasn't all that qualified as I'd only been there a year, so I couldn't really speak with authority on the subjects he mentioned … but we got on marvelously!

And so came Bert's first real brush with the world of film. But even so, he had no idea that it would be a business he would soon become so involved with.

Another link with Hay and Bert's future film career came when Bert discovered in later years that his old chum Desmond Llewelyn, who portrayed "Q" in the Bond films, made his debut in Hay's 1939 comedy *Ask a Policeman* as the headless horseman. Llewelyn often chuckled at the memory and revealed that (as he wasn't exactly distinguishable in the role) he held his right index finger (which he had recently broken) with a crick in it so as his friends might spot him.

Whilst Bert appreciates that Hay's comedy style would now be considered "old hat" with modern audiences, he still holds a tremendously soft spot for them, along with his other favorites of the time.

> My dad used to take me to the Hammersmith Broadway, the Gaumont, Regal and the Commodore cinemas in Chiswick regularly — I saw *Gone with the Wind* in the latter for the first time — and I loved it. We affectionately knew it as the "flickers" which was later shortened to the "flicks." There I watched my favorites like Clark Gable, Errol Flynn with his swashbuckling and, in particular, Basil Rathbone as Sherlock Holmes. Jules Verne was another big favorite of mine and I loved the likes of *Around the World in 80 Days* with David Niven. In fact, I was named after him — Albert Jules Luxford. [The Albert was after the King of Belgium, who died in a mountaineering accident in the year I was born.] My mother was a great fan of his, and I became one too— the technology and scientific advances he wrote of were amazing.

I also used to go with my mother on a Sunday afternoon to the Empire Cinema in Chiswick, which was a actually a theater where they put up a screen for that one day, and they ran wildlife films and older films like *The Jazz Singer* with Al Jolson. So I guess you could say I was a bit of a movie buff by my mid-teens.

Unbeknownst to the young Bert, the seeds were now being sown.

The Air Force Years

However, back at the Institute and the "day job," Bert's superior Dr. Griffin prompted him to excel in all aspects of the profession. In his four years at the Institute, Bert became renowned as a fine engineer. But before the fifth year of his "apprenticeship" was completed, he was conscripted into the Royal Air Force.

It was late 1946 when I eventually joined up for my National Service stint with the RAF. They enrolled me into their Padgate training center, and I was subsequently transferred to the engineering center. Halfway through the course, a sergeant instructor started to take an interest in me and asked if I'd been through a course before, as he thought I was rather accomplished for a new recruit. When I explained I'd done four years at the Institute of Automobile Engineers, he replied with some very choice language to say the least!

Well, I've always learnt not to boast too much or speak about one's abilities out of turn. They never asked about my background when they enrolled me, so I never said anything. Perhaps I should have ... but then again, I felt it wouldn't harm to have a refresher course. My sergeant didn't quite appreciate my train of thought! He was, though, a very nice chap.

Bert then moved to Hornchurch in Essex (which was to be his base for several weeks), awaiting posting.

That next posting came just six weeks later when Bert was moved to RAF Horton, where he was to be one of the RAF Ceremonial Guard of Honor.

When the RAF regiments went out, swinging their rifles and so forth for special parades and occasions—that was us!

One day we were called out to a local airstrip to receive Lady Mountbatten, so into the full regalia we dressed and journeyed out to what was really nothing more than a field—there were no glamorous docking gates like we have nowadays. The plane landed in the field and that's where the staircase was wheeled out to.

I was standing near the front as one of the more senior members of the gang. The stairs were, of course, metal and all open. As Lady Mountbatten ventured down the first few steps, a great gust of wind came from nowhere blowing her skirt right up into the air. She didn't flinch, but carried on descending. Once down she shouted across, "I hope you all had a good look, boys."

That was so funny!

The next posting was Bert's most enjoyable period in the RAF, at South Cirencester. He was invited to become an instructor where he had to teach the pilots engineering. Just as some motorists like to have a general knowledge of what is under the bonnet of their cars, it was thought that pilots should have similar knowledge of their aircraft. (Nowadays it would be unheard of as the aircraft are so sophisticated.)

When you think I was teaching people much higher in rank than what I was: pilot officers, lieutenants, even squadron leaders. It amazed me that many didn't even know what made the propellers spin.

I had a bit of an accident one day and crashed one of our training aircraft! We used to use Tiger Moths and Harvards to demonstrate. Every morning we had to conduct a "routine inspection." My particular aircraft was a Tiger Moth, and the engine is actually upside down — the pots are underneath and the sump at the top. So, with Tiger Moths being very light, you needed two people leaning over the tail whilst it is being revved up to do the check without it moving. Unbeknownst to me, my two colleagues (who I thought were on the tail) had disappeared for a cup of tea. So as I revved up, the propeller went down and it started ploughing. And who should be looking out of the window, but the squadron leader!

I managed to get out of it without much trouble, thank goodness.

Bert had been due to leave the RAF after his two-year National Service period in 1948, but the Suez crisis saw a ban on demobilization and he remained with the Force for another nine months or so.

Back in Business

After leaving the Royal Air Force in 1949, Bert took a job at Henley's, a garage on the Great West Road in Chiswick. They didn't have any engineering vacancies, but did have a vacancy in the stores. As Bert was by now married, he was aware of his responsibilities and decided a job was a job, and this was one that interested him — and might have led to other things. (Henley's was Jaguar's main dealership.)

Within a few months, a job popped up at Pullen's, which made cameras and aircraft instruments just a little further along the road — a perfect opening. Bert joined Pullen's and a few short months later they merged with Taylor, Taylor & Hobsons, who manufactured lenses.

> It was there I took my second "apprenticeship" with instrument making, which totally fascinated me and was in many ways a compliment to my days in the RAF.

A change in family circumstances saw Bert apply for and secure a job as an engineer with British Acoustic Films, an instruments company in Shepherd's Bush, West London. There he was asked if he was interested in sound recording.

In those days, the sound was recorded separately to the film and then dubbed onto the film itself later.

> They showed me a GB Calley projection camera, which was used in the cinemas in those days; about six foot high with great cassettes about two foot square. Next was the sound recording camera, which was very large — three foot long, 18 inches high and one foot deep. It was an optical system whereby sound patterns were recorded on the film. This was to be my "baby."

British Acoustic Films was taken over by the Rank Organization (and its Rank Precision Industries division) a short time after Bert's joining.

J. Arthur Rank

J. Arthur Rank, Chairman and subsequently Life President of the Organization, was a name that became synonymous with British film making. A devout Methodist and millionaire in his own right through the family milling business, Rank became involved in films after he ran several religious titles at his Sunday School classes. Soon exhausting the supply, he decided to make more himself.

He formed the Religious Films Society in 1933 and made his first film, *Mastership*. It was completed at Merton Park Studios in one week and cost £2,700.

The film was a great success, but it was never shown commercially.

Further films followed and in 1935 Rank transferred his production to studios in Elstree which were far superior to the facilities on offer at Merton Park.

Meanwhile, in 1934, Rank formed British National Films with Lady Yule, millionairess widow of Jute baron Sir David Yule, who had become active in the film industry in the early 1930s (to "combat boredom," she claimed). The third member of the team was a young producer named John Corfield, and in 1935 they produced a feature entitled *Turn of the Tide*, based on the 1932 novel *Three Fevers* by Leo Walmsey. A fine cast included Wilfred Lawson, Moore Marriott and Geraldine Fitzgerald.

Further films followed, and soon J. Arthur Rank had built an empire that rivaled all other British companies (and indeed, those in Hollywood). He assumed control of Gaumont-British, Gainsborough, Alexander Korda's Denham Studios, Pinewood Studios and Odeon Cinemas and had the most influential and powerful film distribution company outside of North America. He produced some of the finest films of that era of British cinema (*The Red Shoes*, *Great Expectations*, *Oliver Twist*, *Pygmalion*) and also established an animation division, a B-picture business and the famed "Charm School" where the likes of Christopher Lee, Diana Dors, Joan Collins, Roger Moore and Anthony Steel learned the finer points of being film stars. The empire was phenomenal. It so worried Hollywood that even the likes of David O. Selznick moved to form alliances with Rank for fear of being trounced by his invasion of the U.S.—which, in fact, was an unmitigated disaster.

In the late 1940s, however, Britain was plunged into financial crisis as the world was encountering a massive dollar drain. Hollywood films were a major import and substantial profits were flowing back to American producers. And so the British Government introduced the *ad volerum* tax, imposing a duty of 75 percent on American films in Britain. Furthermore, the tax was payable on "predicted earnings" in advance of release.

The Americans reacted swiftly and an embargo was introduced, preventing any new American films playing in Britain.

The ill-informed government believed that without American dominance, British film makers would be in a much stronger position. But they didn't have the capacity to fill the massive void left. Rank put his film division into overdrive and announced plans for 47 features with an investment of £10 million.

However, before the program could get up to speed, in March 1948, Harold Wilson (President of the Board of Trade) reached a new agreement with the Motion Picture Association of America and the embargo was lifted, just as the first of Rank's films was released. There was a massive influx of American films that had been piling up, and cinemagoers opted for the much more lavish Hollywood product. Rank was plummeted towards financial disaster. At the end of the 1947-48 financial year, the Organization's overdraft was £16 million.

Rank's Managing Director, John Davis, realized that if the Organization was to survive, it would have to diversify and trim down.

Hundreds of jobs were axed. Those who managed to survive found 10 percent was cut from their salary.

Records

Rank diversified considerably: It invested heavily in Xerox, holidays and leisure interests, electronic equipment (Bush radio and television), precision instruments (lenses and cameras) and even records.

Yes, Rank decided they would go up against the likes of EMI in setting up a record division. They therefore advertised for an engineer to open up and run the Rank Audio Plastics division, a job which I applied for.

The production manager there was Peter Shrubshall, who had come over from EMI. Stanley Mather was the chief engineer. Both were charming men and later took me under their wing. Although I admitted to having a very limited knowledge of record manufacturing, that surprisingly didn't bother them. They were setting up to manufacture what they called "flimsy discs" rather than the brittle standard records, and as such weren't looking for a typical record engineer. This was a relatively new process and they wanted a fresh face with fresh ideas.

Peter explained that the idea of the flimsy disc was so that they could be given away free with magazines, catalogues and the like. It all sounded very interesting.

They then showed me the two manufacturing machines. All one had to do was to feed a piece of the flimsy plastic through, into a heat chamber, and at the end you had the two matrices which stamped out two seven-inch records at a time.

There was another company manufacturing flimsy discs but I was told that whereas Rank had the two machines, this other company (Ben Gunn) only had one, so we could manufacture twice the amount at a much more realistic price. In fact, they looked to produce between 600 and 800 a day.

The job was mine, on condition I went to the company in France, just outside Paris, which made the machines that pressed the discs, for a few days. As part of my brief I was to maintain and service the machines as well as run them, I needed to be fully conversant with the workings and assembly.

In fact, I was there for about eight days in all and was treated extremely well; the Rank name carried a certain amount of prestige around Europe, you see.

I went on to press over a million of these discs—which cost a fraction of a penny each—and was awarded two separate silver discs. In those days, for every half-million pressed, the operator was presented with a silver disc much like nowadays when pop groups sell a certain amount of CDs. I'm very proud of my silver discs, which I still have.

Some of the most popular titles included fairy tales such as *Cinderella* along with more serious pieces like the story of John Paul Getty, Sr. One particular topic however, resulted in legal complications.

A book was published with about six of these discs included and one was called "The Heart Beat" and it was quite literally a person's heart beating. We printed hundreds of these things, before some bright spark informed us that we should not print it at all, the reason being that whoever recorded the heart beating never obtained written permission from the person whose heart was used! And because there was no detail on file of who it was, they couldn't be traced—all I knew was that the heart occasionally missed a beat! Not much to go on, but that was my first experience of copyright law—rather bizarre to say the least. So the discs were never released, although I do still have one myself!

One commission for a flimsy disc came through the BBC. In the 1950s, a popular children's radio program was called *Listen with Mother*. The setup was basically an elderly lady, accompanied by a gentleman on a piano, who would tell a story or play a game on air; it was immensely popular.

They asked us to record a session for disc, so off I went with Peter Shrubshall as an observer because I thought it might be fun.

At the BBC studio, I sat back and watched. Off they went with the recording. "Good afternoon, children. Today we're going to play a game. We're going to play a hiding and finding game with your balls.' The piano went plonk and sniggers came from all corners. But the poor innocent old lady had no idea what she was actually saying, and went on. "Take your two balls and with the left hand throw your left ball over your right shoulder, and your right ball over your left …"

We were in hysterics and the pianist was decidedly out of tune with tears running down his cheeks. Needless to say, it was banned from transmission and release!

Pinewood Studios

The Luxford family's move further west to Hillingdon, in the mid–1950s, made commuting a little tricky. Furthermore, the record initiative was floundering as Rank couldn't compete with the giants such as HMV and EMI. With that in mind, Bert decided that it was perhaps time to look for a job a little more local to his new family home.

> My wife saw an advert in the local newspaper which stated that Pinewood Studios was looking for an engineer. As the company I was working for was owned by the Rank Organization, I thought I would effectively be applying for a transfer within the same company, but at a different base, and one nearer to home. That appealed to me.
> I must make it clear that I was just an engineer then, I was not an effects man, nor was I applying to become part of the effects department at the studio; that came a little later.

Bert applied for and secured the position, and along with it his transfer to the world-famous Pinewood Studios (just 15 minutes drive from Hillingdon).

Pinewood Studios opened in 1936 after J. Arthur Rank joined forces with wealthy building tycoon Charles Boot. Their vision was to create a world-class film studio to rival the very best that could be found in Hollywood.

The site for their studio was a former country house called Heatherden Hall in leafy Iver Heath, now just a few minutes drive from the main West London motorway networks, and just 20 minutes drive from Heathrow Airport.

The Hall itself had a fascinating history; most notably, it was the venue for the ratification of the Irish Free State treaty in 1921. In fact, there were many political events and meetings at the Hall as its owner Lt. Col. Grant Morden was himself a member of Parliament. He lavished some £300,000 on the Hall and its 100 acres of grounds adding a 76' ballroom, installing the first privately owned indoor swimming pool, Turkish bathroom, glass-covered squash and tennis courts, and importing rare species of flowers and trees for the ornamental gardens from the Himalayas, Japan, Canada, India, Australia and other far and exotic parts of the world.

Pinewood Studios main entrance. (Gareth Owen Collection.)

Charles Boot bought the house and grounds for a mere £35,000 in 1934 after Morden had died bankrupt.

The ballroom was soon transformed into a luxurious restaurant with its French windows opening onto the gardens, bedrooms turned into first-class suites and a country club established.

Over the next year or so, the site was transformed into a film studio, with a new soundstage being completed every three weeks. The library and ballroom of the Hall was decorated with oak paneling from the SS *Mauritania* (sister ship of the *Lusitania*) and a new Tudor lodge entrance was constructed. To this day it remains the studio's main entrance, and has appeared in countless films.

The studio incorporated every modern feature available: portable remote control switchboards on stages operating cameras, doors, ventilation, telephones and warning lights; power lines into the gardens; its own generators and water supply; lavish dressing rooms and offices.

As the years went on, Pinewood expanded further and gained a first-class global reputation for film production. It also became the home of James Bond and the *Carry On* films.

Earl

The aforementioned John Davis, Managing Director of the Rank Organization, had installed Earl St. John at the studios as "Executive Producer."

Canadian-born St. John was formally "head of exploitation" for Paramount in London; after the Rank-owned Odeon cinema chain bought out Paramount, St. John became personal assistant to Davis. A robust, lovable character, St. John went on to oversee 121 films at the studio and often proved the buffer between the "dreaded" John Davis and organization staff and artists.

> I didn't have a great deal to do with Earl, but certainly knew of him as he was an important figure at Pinewood. He was generally held in a great deal of affection, unlike his boss who wasn't really liked, but then again I don't suppose he was around to be liked!
>
> There was a lovely story about Earl which involved a young, new starter in the editing rooms. On his first day he was told to book the theater for a viewing at 3:30 P.M. This he did. At 3:15 the editor sent him off down to the theater with a couple of cans of film. When he arrived, there was a film being run. He had a word with the projectionist who said they'd be another half-hour or so. Fair enough, he thought, and trotted on back to the editing rooms.
>
> His boss was furious. "You booked the theater, didn't you?" he said.
>
> "Yes," replied the boy.
>
> "Right, in that case, phone the theater and tell whoever is in there to get out!"
>
> So the boy picked up the phoned and dialed the extension. It was answered the other end with a sharp grunt.
>
> "This is the cutting room here. We've booked the theater for 3:30 and would like to ask you to leave now, please."
>
> "What?" came the reply
>
> "Leave, please."
>
> "Do you know who you're talking to?" asked the voice.
>
> "No," said the boy.
>
> "This is Earl St. John."
>
> The boy knew exactly who St. John was!
>
> "Oh ... well, do you know who this is?" he asked.
>
> "No," replied St. John.
>
> "Thank heavens for that," and he slammed the phone down. Lovely!

In Films — At Last!

Once Bert was installed in his new position, several years passed uneventfully within the engineering department and Bert served the studio and its productions in many general capacities. Then, in the early 1960s, Bert was asked to do some direct work on a Walt Disney film, *The*

Horse Without a Head. In the film, some stolen money is hidden in a toy horse, and the crooks who try to retrieve it clash with the police in excellent scenes set on trains and in a toy factory. Leo McKern, Jean-Pierre Aumont and Herbert Lom starred.

I wasn't an effects man then either, but worked purely as an engineer. I had several jobs on the picture — mainly mechanical — which the art director would ask me to complete. I can't say they were particularly glamorous or exciting jobs, but it was a very enjoyable experience. If a door needed to slam — without anyone in view — or if we needed a window to break ... that sort of thing. They weren't really "special effects" in the sense of what I did in later films, but all the same, they had to be achieved!

The interesting, and indeed important, thing about [Walt] Disney was that he was the first major renter of studio space at Pinewood. That is to say, up until his coming to the studio its output was virtually all "Rank Organization" films. After all, Rank had a marvelous production program and could fill the studio with those pictures all year round. But when things started to slow down a bit, "renters" were welcomed.

Disney's arrival caused a few hiccups at the studio, just as any new influence does. Little things like them wanting their own car park area were pooh-poohed because, it was felt, that everyone who worked at the studio would then want a reserved parking space and it would cause chaos. Mmmm. Silly really, I know. Then when Disney's production manager — Peter Manley — said he wanted a refreshments trolley on the stage for two hours every morning and afternoon for cast and crew (saving them marching off to the canteen and claiming back expenses and the like), the Managing Director of the studio, Kip Herren, almost had a fit.

"You can't do that," he exclaimed, "as it will set a precedent for all productions, Rank and otherwise. Not only that, you'll have people from other stages wandering in taking advantage and drinking your tea. Oh, no, we can't have that."

It sounds daft, I know, but that was the attitude. Peter Manley stood firm and reminded Kip that Disney was going to spend an awful lot of money at the studio. He also suggested that he might have a lady on the payroll to run the refreshment trolley, and she would keep an eye on who was and who wasn't entitled to partake the hospitality of Walt Disney. That swung it.

A lovely little lady called Margaret, from the canteen, was charged with looking after the trolley, as she had a very good memory for faces. After a few days, she pretty well knew who was on the Disney unit and who wasn't. Anyone caught sneaking in from neighboring production for a cuppa were swiftly chastised and sent packing!

Bert and a model helicopter he made for the exciting mountain top chase finale between Bond and SPECTRE in *From Russia with Love*.

Anyway, one afternoon this chap wandered onto the stage, looked around and went over to Margaret, requesting a cup of coffee.

"Oh no you don't," she said. "You're not on the unit, so scram."

"But I am with the unit," he replied.

"Oh, no you're not — I haven't seen you here before, and I know them all on this unit."

"But I am with them," he insisted.

"What's your name?" she inquired.

With all modesty, he introduced himself to Margaret:

"I'm Walt Disney," he said.

Dear old Margaret nearly fainted.

"Oooh, oooh, dear ... oooh..." she went on, obviously realizing her big mistake.

Walt Disney went over to Peter Manley, who had heard the exchange, and said:

"Peter, that lady over there ..."

"Yes, Walt?"

"She's marvelous—look after her!"

Disney obviously appreciated that little Margaret was looking after his interests, and was very appreciative. I love that story!

Bert's involvement in the film was to lead to greater things, with many of the subsequent productions based at Pinewood. His later move into special effects proper wasn't really an accident, but by the same token it wasn't really planned either; it was more of a drift than a conscious career move. However, he soon became noted for his ingenuity, meticulous attention to detail and reliability.

His apprenticeship (or perhaps more appropriately, his baptism of fire) was now seemingly served. He was about to become involved more and more in the gimmick side of production, although still essentially as an engineer.

After returning to his department, Bert was called upon to work on another little film, this one called *Dr. No.*

There weren't really many "special effects" on the film, just like *Horse Without a Head*— we had the nuclear reactor room with different radiation detecting machines, the "elevator platform" descending into the liquid on which Bond and Dr. No fight it out, the Dragon tank which was basically a flame thrower effect, gunfire and ricocheting ... all pretty straightforward stuff again.

Bert's mechanical engineering effects were just that, mechanical. The flashing lights, moving dials and firearms, etc., fell to other departments.

Special effects are brought about by a team, a very big team, and that must always be remembered. Although the effects on this film were what might be called incidental, mechanical and (to a lesser extent) visual, it was a particularly difficult yet brilliant film to work on. I had my areas, the other boys had theirs and although we were perhaps working individually, ultimately it was to achieve the same goal.

Nobody knew how successful *Dr. No* would be, though — I'd be lying if I said they did. And when I was working with the different actors during various stages of the film, it was never really suggested or discussed as being anything other than a run-of-the-mill film.

Pinewood's special effects department was then headed by Frank George (uncle of actress Susan George) and Bert learned some very valu-

A UFO used, here seen outside Bert's workshop.

able lessons about effects and processes involved therein from him, for now he found himself becoming increasingly involved in this specialized area.

> Frank would say, "Bert, if you can pull it with a bit of string, pull it — don't put an engine at the end of it if you don't have to!" Simplicity is the true art of effects.

It was a lesson Bert heeded and one which he passes on to this day, in the world of computerized gimmickry and miracles.

Colleagues

> There were a few others around the department too: Jimmy Snow, Cliff Richardson, Bill Warrington and a lovely chap by the name of Sid Pearson. I guess you could say, like Frank George, Sid was one of the "originals" at Pinewood — his background was in chemistry, as a matter of fact, when he worked for Glaxo — and he became very much

involved in the explosives side of the business. He was affectionately known as "Seagull Sid" around the studio on account of an incident with the aforementioned feathered bird. On a picture, he was asked to spray a seagull pink. It was all very harmless dye he used, and wasn't cruel, I must add — but the bird wasn't keen, to say the least! They then had to take the bird on location down on the coast, where the seagull was tied by one foot to a length of nylon. When Sid's back was turned, the bird slipped the knot and flew off to the top of a cliff. Dear old Sid gave chase and managed to get to the cliff with the bird still there. He climbed around the top edge, popped his head over and then — wham! The seagull gave him a very nasty bite on the top of his nose. It must have been very painful because Sid spouted some rather choice words at the bird.

I've mentioned that Sid was involved in explosives, but what I didn't say was that each and every time he was, he tried to make his explosions bigger and better than the last. I remember he was asked to blow a little bridge (made of balsa wood) which had been built over the pond at Pinewood, and, boy, did he blow it up. In one frame it was there, in the next it had vanished. The bang reverberated right around the studio and it took out some windows on the houses in Pinewood Road opposite the studio.

To put it in perspective, and to be fair to Sid, in those days the effects business was really in its infancy, so there was a lot of hit and miss, trial and error involved; and that is how the business developed. Sid didn't exactly miss, but his hits were fine-tuned in later assignments!

All in the department became distinguished in their field — in particular, Bill Warrington, Cliff Richardson and, a little later, John Stears.

Bill Warrington "debuted" in 1944's *The Way Ahead* and progressed to films such as *The Planters Wife*, directed by Ken Annakin, Ronald Neame's *The Card*, the comedy *An Alligator Named Daisy* (in which he was involved in making a mechanical working alligator after the real one became too frisky to handle), Lewis Gilbert's *Reach for the Sky*, the superb *Titanic* dramatization *A Night to Remember*, *The Guns of Navarone* and, just before his death in 1981, *Raiders of the Lost Ark* (the first of the Indiana Jones films).

Cliff Richardson had started out a year before Bill Warrington with *The Bells Go Down*, but was soon working with distinguished filmmakers of the day including John Huston (*The African Queen*) and David Lean (*Lawrence of Arabia*). He even worked with the Beatles on *Help!* before moving on to *A Funny Thing Happened on the Way to the Forum, Battle of*

Bert, John Stears and Joe Fitt.

Britain, The Day of the Jackal and *The Mackintosh Man*. His young son John went on to emulate his father's success.

John Stears

Regarded as one of Britain's foremost effects experts, John Stears and his close-knit team of Bert Luxford, Frank George, Jimmy Snow, Joe Fitt (prop man and effects) and Charlie Dodds (effects rigger) became the "dream team" and Stears was nicknamed the "Dean of Effects."

From starting out working on TV with *Dr. Who*, Stears transferred to films at Pinewood in 1962 and worked on the first six Bond adventures: blowing up the bauxite mine in *Dr. No*, the SPECTRE helicopters in *From Russia with Love* and the Disco Volante in *Thunderball*, amongst other (greater) things.

Yes, John loved blowing things up. It was like playtime for him and he never grew out of it. But then again, if you were having as much fun as we were, why "grow up"?

He did a lot of model work too and later, on the Bond films and specifically *You Only Live Twice*, he was heavily involved in the space sequences which was rather fortuitous as he later went on to work on *Star Wars* and snared his second Oscar; his first came with *Thunderball*, although he didn't even know he'd been nominated … until the statuette arrived.

Bert and John Stears' partnership lasted from the first Bond film through to Roger Moore's first two outings some 12 years later, and was undoubtedly the period remembered most fondly by Bert.

Stears died in 1999 at the age of 65 after suffering a massive and sudden brain hemorrhage in California, after working on *The Mask of Zorro* with Antonio Banderras and Anthony Hopkins.

All of Bert's colleagues were highly regarded amongst the effects community. Bert worked closely with both Frank George and Jimmy Snow, but it was perhaps his association with John Stears and Cliff Richardson that yielded some of his finest work.

They were all a brilliant bunch of chaps, and we had great fun together. So many happy memories, so many great friends.

SCENE THREE

The Bond Years

Bert Luxford was undoubtedly the most brilliant engineer in John Stears' effects team.

He was largely responsible for bringing to life my designs for some of the gadgetry. Nothing was too difficult for him and the word "impossible" did not exist in his vocabulary.

He cares more about his work rather than the limelight of publicity and I was always struck by his modesty.

For me, Bert is the personification of the true "back room boy" and someone for whose technical skills I will always have the greatest admiration.

— Ken Adam, Production Designer

A series of films based on British writer Ian Fleming's hero James Bond had been mooted by several potential producers ever since Fleming's first book was published in 1953. *Casino Royale*, his first 007 adventure, had been staged as a live CBS broadcast for *Climax* in 1954, with Barry Nelson as "Jimmy Bond." It was a one-off deal that Fleming later regretted; the story was subsequently given the feature film treatment in 1967 by Charles K. Feldman as a spoof — more on that later.

However, it wasn't until the early 1960s that the film series got off the drawing board when American producer Albert R. Broccoli expressed a desire to film the stories. He had previously expressed an interest but his then-production partner Irving Allen wasn't keen on the subject matter.

The Bond producers (left) Harry Saltzman and (right) Albert R. "Cubby" Broccoli.

Broccoli learned that an option had been taken on the stories by Canadian producer Harry Saltzman, but the option was soon to expire.

Saltzman had been unsuccessful in arranging finance, but Broccoli had good connections back in L.A., so the pair decided to work together and formed Eon Productions.

A meeting was arranged with Broccoli, Saltzman and Arthur Krim at United Artists, after which the producers walked away with a multi-picture deal for a series of films. *Dr. No* was the first in that series with a relatively unknown Scottish actor in the lead role: Sean Connery.

It's quite amusing to think, as my friend Eunice Gayson recently reminded me, that Sean almost messed it all up in what is probably one of the most famous scenes in film history.

He and Eunice [as Sylvia Trench] had the scene together at the Chemin de Fer table in the casino. If you remember, Eunice says that she needs another "fifty" and Sean says, "I admire your courage, Miss …?" Eunice replies, "Trench, Sylvia Trench. I admire your luck, Mister…?" Now, all Sean had to say was "Bond, James Bond." But could he do it? No!

Sean was very nervous about landing the part of Bond and prior to shooting decided that he would not drink at all, to keep his mind totally clear.

The first exciting scene in *Dr. No* when Bond is introduced to the cinema-going public (Connery plays opposite Eunice Gayson as Sylvia Trench).

So, when it came to his line, his nerves obviously got the better of him as he said

"Bond, Sean Bond ... oh, damn, can we go again?"

Take Two.

"Connery, James ... damn!"

Take Three

"James, James Bond ... damn it!"

To cut a long story short, by the time they had reached take 18 the director had his head in his hands and the

Desmond Llewelyn, Little Nellie and Sean Connery.

producers were looking at each other as if to say "What have we done?"

Eunice tactfully suggested that they take a break and suggested Sean might take a little drink with her to calm his nerves. When they returned, he tried again:

"Bond, James Bond"—word perfect. But then, Eunice fluffed her next line, would you believe. She'd been word perfect for 18 takes and then couldn't get it out. It was so funny.

One of the final sequences in the film was one in which Bert had a hand: Dr. No's bauxite mine and docks had to blown up as Bond and Honey (Ursula Andress) escape. I worked on building the model of the docks with Jimmy and John Stears. It created a lovely mess. That was really John's first involvement with the Bonds. Frank George was the effects man on the film out in Jamaica. Granted there weren't many effects, but we did have gunfire, blowing up a car going over a cliff, the dragon tank and so on; it wasn't insignificant. John then, in the next film, really took over from Frank.

The explosion of the bauxite mine made another appearance in *From Russia with Love*, which you probably won't have heard about …

The Attaché Case

The massive success of the first James Bond adventure prompted a sequel, swiftly put into preparation. *From Russia with Love* (which President John F. Kennedy had named one of his favorite books) was Connery's second and perhaps definitive portrayal of Her Majesty's most famous secret agent. It saw Bert's involvement increase considerably—in fact, more than doubling that on his last two assignments combined.

007 crew badges. (Robin Harbour.)

From Russia with Love is probably my favorite Bond film as I think I did more work on it—with the possible exception of the Aston Martin DB5 in *Goldfinger*—than on any other film, and because it was, in a way, my introduction to the big films and the bigger effects!

As previously mentioned, the famous attaché case came about when art director Syd Cain approached Bert with a rough sketch.

Rough is the word. The sketches usually came on a little bit of paper, very un-detailed and mostly very vague, and with little time to realize them. Don't get me wrong, I have the greatest respect for art directors like Syd Cain, and production designer Ken Adam, but their work, in a way, is theoretical; mine is practical. I have to try and take their ideas and turn them into working prototypes, and back then we didn't have computers or sophisticated electronics— it was all mechanical. You must remember that the Bond films were always ahead of their time, and so were the designers' ideas.

In *Russia*, Syd wanted the attaché case to have a knife that popped out, which was fairly easy, we used a spring and release catch. The turnable catches, again, fairly easy. But the tear gas canister wasn't quite that straightforward.

Peter Hunt was editor on this one, as he was on *Dr. No*, and Peter has a wicked sense of humor. Now comes the bauxite dock explosion I mentioned. Peter had been told that the top brass from United Artists were coming over to Pinewood for a screening of the rough cut so far. So Peter thought he'd have a bit of fun.

There they were, all sitting in the theater watching the first couple of reels and we reached the Q-Bond scene with the attaché case. Q explained the operation and told Bond to try, being sure to turn the catches through 90 degrees. As Sean did it and popped the catch, Peter Hunt cut directly to the explosion of the bauxite docks and pulled up "The End" credits. The UA people stared in horror. Meanwhile Terence Young had fell off his seat, wetting himself with laughter. He thought it was hilarious! For years afterwards he kept that print and revelled at showing it as a "party piece."

In the film, Bond's life hangs in the balance when, just before an amazingly staged fight between him and Robert Shaw's SPECTRE heavy-man Grant, he is held at gunpoint and told how he will suffer a slow, agonizing and humiliating death in a carriage aboard the Orient Express. Two briefcases lie in the compartment, one belonging to Bond and the other stolen by Grant from MI6 operative Capt. Nash (who was played by the film's production manager Bill Hill after the chosen actor for the part fell ill), whom Grant had then impersonated to win Bond's confidence.

Bond offers to buy Grant out by doubling what the Russians are paying. Uninterested, Grant declines. Bond asks for, and then offers to buy, a cigarette with the sovereigns in his attaché case. Curious as to whether Nash's case contains a similar wealth, Grant proceeds to open it, making

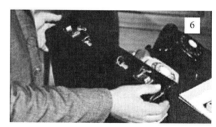

1. The attaché case Bert made for *From Russia with Love.* The next eight images are the gadgets Bert incorporated in the attaché case, as seen in the film; 2. folding sniper's rifle; 3. the gold sovereigns; 4. the throwing knife; 5. the throwing knife II; 6. the exploding stun gas I (showing how the locks have to be turned to activate it; 7. stun gas II; 8. stun gas III; 9. stun gadget.

the fatal mistake of not turning the catches through 90 degrees. As he lifts the lid, the tear gas canister explodes and thus provides Bond with a chance to reverse the gunpoint scenario.

> The explosion was actually achieved when I squirted some oil into a gun, a pipe from which was fed through into the case and *whoompf*— harmless oil smoke, but with the desired effect.
>
> I've already mentioned how Desmond Llewelyn in his first appearance as Q presented Bond with the case, but there was an interesting little story behind that scene. Desmond was, of course, a Welshman and a few years earlier had appeared in a film for Terence Young who was directing *Russia*. It was called *They Were Not Divided* and in it Desmond played a Welsh tank driver with a broad Welsh accent.
>
> When he arrived on set for his scene in *Russia*, Terence asked him how he was going to play the character. Desmond said that he saw the character as a typical English civil servant and would play him with his ordinary English accent and mannerisms.
>
> Terence was appalled at the suggestion and said that he must play him as a Welshman. Desmond hesitated for a moment and said, "Terence do you honestly want me to say [Adopting a ridiculously strong Welsh accent], "Well, now, see, here's a *loverly* little case I've got for you and if you press here out pops a knife, see ..."
>
> Terence shook his head and said, "No, you're quite right, old chap. An Englishman it is to be."

Earlier in the film, as early as the pre-title sequence in fact, Bert's gimmicks were in evidence.

> The opening scene, set in the gardens at Pinewood, sees Robert Shaw stalking "Bond" through the hedgerows. When he eventually comes across "Bond," he pulls a garrotte wire out of his watch and ... snap! He was later revealed to be a look a like and not the real 007, though. The watch was just a standard wristwatch, with a coiled spring and wire inside.
>
> Actually, that sequence had to be re-shot in part — when the rubber mask was removed from the actor who was playing the Bond double, he looked almost like Sean Connery! Unfortunately, it wasn't noticed until rushes the following day and so editor Peter Hunt assembled a tiny crew and shot an insert of another actor (with a mustache) in the "revealing" shot. Peter also shot some other inserts of Sean and Robert Shaw's feet as they crossed the bridge, adding further suspense to the opening.

Black Park, here snow covered. (Courtesy Robin Harbour.)

The garrotte watch wasn't necessarily a new invention, as previous unsavory use was allegedly made by Russian and Spanish agents.

The Lektor

Bert's greatest challenge, however, came when Syd Cain described the Lektor decoding device to him.

> There wasn't even a sketch with it! Syd just explained that he needed this machine, probably square in shape, and about the size of a typewriter as it needed to be portable. The rest was down to me, and I pretty much had free rein.
> What does a decoding machine look like, I wondered? Nobody knew.
> I made the machine with all sorts of cogs, wheels and drums that went round. It's only on screen for a few minutes but everyone was terribly pleased with it, and my design; it looked just like a decoder probably should and would.
> What I found with Syd, and the great Ken Adam who designed so

The Lektor decoding device Bert constructed for *From Russia with Love.*

many of the best Bond sets, was that they were brilliant visualists, and would say, "We see this thing looking a bit like so and so, and doing these actions…" It was then down to me to take their lead.

Adam and Cain

Undoubtedly this creative duo had the greatest influence on Bert's film career, as well as being acclaimed geniuses in their own right.

Adam, who was actually born in Germany, entered films as an assistant in the art department on films such as *Captain Horatio Hornblower, The Crimson Pirate* and *Helen of Troy* and progressed quickly through the ranks as art director and production designer on the likes of *Night of the Demon, The Trails of Oscar Wilde* and *Last Days of Soddom and Gomorah.* It was through working with Cubby Broccoli on *The Trials of Oscar Wilde* that he was recommended for the role of production designer on *Dr. No.* He brought a fresh, innovative and colorful style to the film. The budget was tight (Adam was told his entire art department total was just £14,000 — he stretched it to £21,000 by the end of shooting). Adam's work was nothing short of extraordinary — the reactor room set, the Crab Key waiting area and the eerie undersea living room were highly acclaimed. Other sets belied their actual cost and it was unquestionably Adam's distinctive look coupled with Terence Young's brilliant direction and Peter Hunt's editing that led to *Dr. No* being a triumph on the screen.

Adam returned for six further Bond adventures: *Goldfinger, Thunderball, You Only Live Twice* (during which he constructed the immense volcano set on the Pinewood back lot), *Diamonds Are Forever, The Spy Who Loved Me* (building the world's largest stage, the 007 stage, at Pinewood) and *Moonraker.*

Adam was Oscar-nominated for several Bond films, but went on to win for *Barry Lyndon* (1975) and *The Madness of King George* (1994).

Meanwhile, back in the 1960s, Syd Cain assumed the role of Adam's art director on *Dr. No,* having similarly started off as assistant art director in the industry: on *Cockleshell Heroes* (1955). His

Production designer Ken Adam OBE — Bert's inspiration.

debuting film as art director was the Bob Hope–Bing Crosby comedy *Road to Hong Kong*; he then joined Adam for the first Bond film. When Adam proved unavailable for the next adventure (*From Russia with Love*) due to his involvement with Stanley Kubrick's *Dr. Strangelove,* Cain assumed production designer chores. He did it again in *On Her Majesty's Secret Service* (1969) and was supervising art director on Roger Moore's debut Bond, *Live and Let Die* (1973). He later returned in 1995 as storyboard artist for *Goldeneye,* Pierce Brosnan's first 007 adventure. Other film credits included *The Wild Geese, The Sea Wolves, Who Dares Wins* (in which he dressed the Pinewood mansion for storming by the SAS) and *Fear Is the Key.*

Footwork

Another gimmick (which lead actress Lotte Lenya to say, "W*henever I go to dinner parties, the first thing people look at are my shoes*") was the wonderful poison tipped blade-popping shoe which Lenya, as Rosa Klebb, used to great effect in the demise of Kronsteen (Vladek Sheybal).

It did actually work and the blade did pop out, although they wouldn't have hurt anyone as they were spring-loaded, I made sure of that. Mind

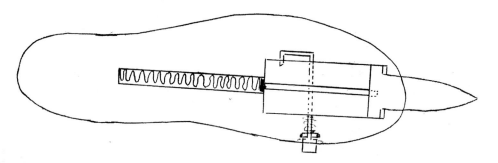

The design for Klebb's shoe, *From Russia with Love.*

Rosa Klebb's (Lotte Lenya's) poison-tipped shoe.

you, the one later shown in exhibitions was, as far as I'm concerned after looking at it, not the original one I made, and I should know. In my sketch you'll note that the blade was the shape of a real knife blade, whereas the supposed "real" shoe has a much wider (at the base) triangular blade.

Bert also worked on the helicopter attack sequence. When Bond shoots the helicopter pilot and the machine spins out of control, hitting the ground and exploding — that was Bert's doing. The helicopter model was, almost as large as Bert.

The film's finale did actually feature a real helicopter crash and almost killed the director. During filming the boat chase sequence in the Scottish

Top and right: Both photographs are scenes from *From Russia with Love.*

Highlands, one of the helicopters filming the action flew out of control and crashed into the Loch, taking Terence Young down with it, and almost injuring many of the leading cast in the process. After swimming to safety, Young brushed himself down and got back to work. Sheer professionalism.

The Midas Touch

From Russia with Love was an overnight success, and the third 007 adventure was all set: *Goldfinger* (1964).

The pre-title sequence sees Bond swim into frame, underwater, with a fake seagull on his head disguising his snorkel.

> I shouldn't laugh, but it was a big joke. I mean, James Bond was a suave, sophisticated agent, and here he is with a bird on his head!
>
> When he gets out of the water, he fires a grappling gun up over a wall, from which a rope shot and was supposed to be secured via the grappling hook on top of the wall so as he could pull himself up and over. Once his mission is over, he strips off his "dry suit" to reveal a white-jacketed dress suit.
>
> It was rehearsed for three days and all was fine. For the take, it was night and we were on the tank at Pinewood. Sean came out of the water and fired the gun; but it didn't fire! It was pneumatically controlled, and the air just didn't go through. The wardrobe man starting laughing his head off and shouted, "It hasn't worked, has it?" The director, Guy Hamilton, came over and said, "Hang on a moment, we haven't finished yet. Right, shall we do it again?" Sean, being the professional gentleman he is, did it again without quibble, and it worked perfectly. He pulled himself over the wall and then proceeded to take his dry suit off (it was shot in this order, although in the film he removed his dry suit a little later after blowing up the plant). When he did, his supposedly white jacket was quite black! Wardrobe had dropped a clanger.
>
> Guy then said, 'Can we do it again please, Sean, because your dry suit is now a wet suit?' Sean wasn't best pleased, and everyone else laughed at the wardrobe man. He never spoke out of turn again. He knew nothing about my job, but made fun when it didn't quite go to plan and I hate that.

A Glint in the Eye

Another interesting sequence in the opening is where Bond returns to a hotel room, in which a young lady is waiting for him. Unbeknownst to him, there's a thug lurking too.

> Sean is kissing the young lady and in her eye sees the reflection of the thug (Alf Joint) approaching with a cosh, and so he has time to turn the situation around — quite literally.
>
> That reflection was done by matte painting which is a process whereby you "add" to a picture, or frame(s) of film in this case, by physically painting it in. Cliff Culley, a very talented matte artist at Pinewood, created that shot, and it's marvelously effective. Watch it closely next time you see the film. It's a very clever shot.

Another young lady who made a big impression in the film was Shirley Eaton. Hers became one of the most famous scenes in the film, and Shirley became one of the most photographed actresses of the 1960s. It was of course the scene where her character (Jill Masterson) assisted Bond in humiliating Auric Goldfinger, who was cheating at cards. She was discovered by Bond (after he was knocked unconscious by henchman Oddjob) on his bed, painted from head to toe in gold paint. Although Shirley's appearance lasted less than five minutes, it is for those five minutes she is most famously remembered.

The DB5

Bert's most demanding (and perhaps most satisfying) assignment on the film was with the legendary Aston Martin DB5 — dubbed "The Most Famous Car in the World."

That was a job and a half. One person could never, ever have coped with that car. It was a team of four people, actually. John Stears was the director of effects on the film. He was very good, but his background was in model-making, not engineering. He said, "We've got to have these over-riders coming out, the bulletproof shield at the back, the revolving number plates and the ejector seat." I myself was in charge of the over-riders, machine guns and the rear bulletproof screen. That was enough, as we only had three months.

There was nothing electronic in those days, it was all mechanical. We had hydraulic tanks in the boot running all the gimmicks. If you've ever been in an Aston, you'll know there isn't much room anyway, so for us to pack all of these things in there was no mean feat.

The features of the DB5 included:

- an ejector seat, controlled by a button hidden in the top of the gear stick
- a weapons control panel in the center arm rest, controlling:
  - revolving tire slashers as concealed in the hub of the front wheels
  - front-mounted machine guns hidden behind the front indicator lights
  - revolving license plates valid in England, Switzerland and France
  - oil spray, smoke screen and nail dispenser behind rear lights (the nails were not featured in the film)
  - a rear bulletproof shield
  - hydraulic over-riders, front and back

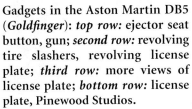

Gadgets in the Aston Martin DB5 (*Goldfinger*): *top row:* ejector seat button, gun; *second row:* revolving tire slashers, revolving license plate; *third row:* more views of license plate; *bottom row:* license plate, Pinewood Studios.

• a weapons tray under the driver's seat
• a mobile phone in a compartment in the driver's door
• a radar tracking system hidden behind the radio speaker

Before filming could get underway, there was one minor problem that had to be resolved:

The DB5 had to go back the factory at Newport Pagnell because the clutch had burnt out! It was only a tiny clutch, for such a big car, and that became a common problem. It wasn't a new car when we were "loaned" it; in fact, it had been around for a while as a test car. It then came back to Pinewood all set for the first night of filming.

The shoot was in the "Goldfinger factory" which was actually the alleyways around Pinewood's stores department.

Sean was driving — well, no, it wasn't Sean, it was really Bob Simmons the stunt man, and the script called for the car to approach a large mirror which reflected its headlights, looking like an approaching car, and Bond was to crash into a fake wall after he couldn't see a way out. What Bob didn't know was that whereas the wall was false, behind it lay the footworks of buildings and scaffolding. And he drove into the wall with quite a force. It smashed the front of the car in — after our three months of hard work! It was an accident, and wasn't his fault, I realize that. But for it to happen on the first night was criminal. The car had to go back to the factory again!

There were now two Aston Martin DB5s: the gimmick car and the "road car" which was used for most of the driving sequences. (The gimmick car was not considered too roadworthy with the many modifications, although when the "road car" broke down, the gimmick car was used!) The most exciting of the modifications, and possibly the most anticipated in the film, was the ejector seat.

The ejector seat actually worked. It was built by Jimmy Ackland-Snow and was triggered with highly compressed air.

In the film, Bond passed through a security gate with a little old lady looking after it; that was down on the Pinewood lot near the plasterers' shop. Soon afterwards, Bond pressed the button on the gear stick and the ejector seat engaged.

It was fired by remote control, without anyone in the car. It worked perfectly. The top of the roof flew off and the seat went whoosh. It was all over in about four seconds, and a mannequin was used — not a real body, as nobody could have survived that!

Jimmy did a good job of the seat. He also worked on the revolving

The ejector seat in action in the Aston Martin DB5 in *Goldfinger*.

number plates but they weren't quite as satisfactory. Unlike Frank George, who was an electronic man and who would have had it all done with electrics and buttons, Jimmy opted to use cables. So whenever we wanted the plates to revolve, we had to pull a lever.

It was a lovely car, though!

Desmond Llewelyn's portrayal of Q was honed to a fine art during this third Bond adventure.

When Sean first enters Q-branch, he sees a few gadgets being demonstrated and crosses to Desmond, who is at a workbench. In rehearsals, Desmond stood up to greet Bond, but Guy shouted out, "No, no, you hate this man. He destroys everything you give him!"

That's when Desmond said it all clicked into place. From then on, the character was played with an almost-dislike of Bond and his attitude to all Q's hard work in creating the gadgets. In truth, Q had a soft spot for Bond, but when explaining the functions of the DB5 to him, Bond was clearly wishing he was somewhere else and made quips—especially regarding the ejector seat when he said,

"Ejector seat? You're joking!"

A stony-faced Q replied sharply,

"I never joke about my work, 007."

I did love Desmond because he was *us*—the back room technicians and engineers. He even, in his own way, glamorized our role but did it in such an admirable and semi-serious way as to perfectly reflect our feelings.

Later on in the shoot, Bert and John Stears journeyed to the Aston Martin factory for lunch with the Managing Director.
"You've given us quite a lot of good publicity," the Director said.
"In what way?" asked John.
With that, the chap brought out a large scrapbook which must have been four inches thick.
"This is all the free advertising," he said. "About £3 million worth."
It is, therefore, rather ironic to think that the company later stripped the gimmick car and re-sold it!

I think the only remaining part of the film version car is the number plate, which is a shame. The other road model, and a further two promotional models are still around, as are a few later mock-up replicas.

Mutual Respect

As well as having a tremendous fondness for the FX team at Pinewood, Bert's admiration and respect for his production designer Ken Adam was unquestionable. The same could be said of Adam, where Bert was concerned.
Whereas Bert's work was based very much in the real "engineering" world, to a certain degree Adam's was fantasy world. Had Bert been asked to come up with a few gimmicks for the car without any sketches or outlines, it's pretty certain what would have resulted would be an imaginative yet very practical model. Adam's visualization of the car was anything but practical. Perhaps his lack of engineering background was a bonus? Had he been an engineer, would his design have been as outrageously amazing? Here the engineer and film designer complimented each other, for each drove the other to new, un-thought-of limits, and each was certainly ahead of their time.

The genius in the DB5 was not that every gimmick was new, it wasn't. We'd seen tire-slasher things in *Ben-Hur*, ejector seats in aeroplanes, and machine guns and oil slicks had been used in cars before then, during the American Prohibition period. No, the genius was in bringing it all together in one machine.

Corgi issued a model of the DB5 and it became an instant best-seller complete with ejector seat, over-riders and machine guns. The company went on to sell 2 million of the model cars.

The Bomb

Another assignment for Ken Adam's back room boys came with the atomic bomb which Goldfinger planted inside Fort Knox. The interior of the famous American gold depository was recreated by Adam on one of Pinewood's stages. Although the filmmakers were allowed to film overhead the real Fort Knox, they were not allowed any nearer nor inside. Therefore, Adam recreated exterior on the Pinewood backlot and let his imagination run wild for the interior. He piled gold bars several feet high (which in reality would never be done because of its sheer weight) and made the glittering depository an awesome sight. So much so, he received letters asking as to how he gained permission to film inside. Bert remembers the set vividly:

That blasted bomb was the size of a coffin, made of aluminum, and on wheels. Frank George made the housing which I'll come to a little later; I was responsible for the innards and body.

When I'd completed it, Peter Murton, the art director, came in, looked at what I'd done, and said 'That's very nice, Bert, but can you make it a bit more sexy?'

"Hang on," I said. "How am I supposed to make an atomic bomb sexy?"

"I want a bit more detail in it, things going around, lots of colors— you've got a fortnight, you'll be all right."

I said yes okay, I'll have a go. I was pulling my hair out thinking about what I might do, and then I had a brainwave ... which I've regretted ever since.

Back in my old days as an engineer, we had a thing called engine turning, which you see in very old clocks—you open the front and see all these wonderfully detailed, nice patterns. So I thought I'd do that.

Frank George asked what I was going to do, and I told him that I was thinking about engine turning all the disks in the machine.

"You'll regret it," he said. "Everything will have to be engine-turned from now on after they see this!"

It is a filthy job. It involves carbon, graphite and paraffin and you're up to your neck in the rubbish that spins off. Nevertheless, I finished it and held my breath. Peter Murton came in and said, "That looks great."

"Well, if you want it any more sexy," I said, "I'll pin a picture of Marilyn Monroe on it for you."

"No! That's great," he said.

Frank George, meanwhile, made the little countdown mechanism — which was electronic — and that's what everyone's attention is hooked on in the film; the engine turning wasn't noticed!

Lasers

The film's villain, Auric Goldfinger (played brilliantly by German actor Gert Frobe), gained entry to the highly protected and secured Fort Knox building by means of aerial-spraying the soldiers with poisonous gas (or so he thought), and using a large industrial laser to cut through the thick steel outer doors of the vault.

Actually, the laser beam should have been blue, not orange as it was in the film, and it was an extremely dangerous thing insofar as it having 400 to 500 volts going through the coil (made by Osram). If you touched it, you'd have been dead. It wasn't a toy. If you'd

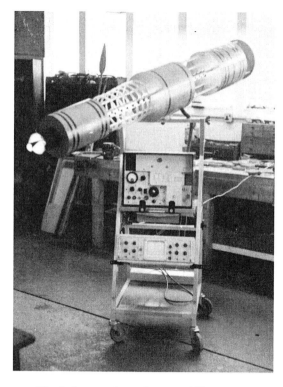

The infamous laser from *Goldfinger*.

gone within a foot of it when it was on, you'd have had arcs too — giving a very nasty shock, to say the least.

Opposite page: The laser table scene from *Goldfinger* where Bond is to be killed.

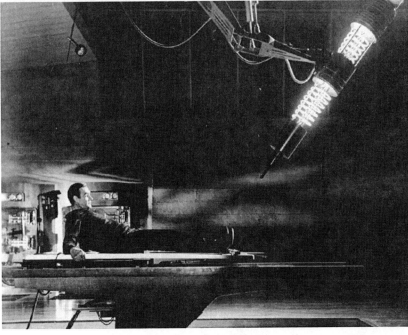

That wasn't the first sight of the laser (which stands for Light Amplification by Stimulated Emission of Radiation) in the film, however, as a laughing Bert Luxford recalled:

> Sean was spread-eagled on Goldfinger's table in that big room, with the laser pointing down at him! It's switched on and the beam (which was added in optically later) started cutting through the table and up towards Sean's crotch.
>
> We had to make it look real, and as though it was cutting through the table. So … [laughter] … I had the job of being under the table with an acetylene torch. The center of the table, through which I was burning, was lead and I just worked my way along it, on my back, once I was given the word. However, as I couldn't really see how far up the table I was, I had to be told when to stop. As I got nearer and nearer to his crotch, Sean was sweating a bit. I hate the thought of ever injuring an actor — but "there" would have been awful!
>
> I followed my cues exactly and was listening to Gert and Sean's dialogue carefully, too, as I knew it would end, and laser switch off, after Sean mentioned "Operation Grandslam." I was about three inches from his crotch when I stopped.

Goldfinger's henchman, a stocky Korean wrestler named Oddjob, was brilliantly played by Harold Sakata. His infamous means of disposing with undesirables: a toss of a steel-rimmed bowler hat, which he threw like a Frisbee.

> We weren't involved with the making of the hat but were involved with the "flying" sequences. We had to put an electric motor in the hat, as when it was thrown the hat was supposed to spin; bowler hats don't spin of their own accord, I assure you, and so we had to rig something up that would do it. The motor worked surprisingly well, as you can see in the film, especially considering the weight of this damn thing, which must have been five or six pounds.
>
> The flight path was prearranged on very fine, strong wires.
>
> In the scene at the golf club where Oddjob throws the hat at a statue, I rigged the wires up there for the initial throw; but on the cut to the statue head, I used the garden at Pinewood with a pre-rigged statue. The hat hit the head, I pressed a button and a little charge caused the head to fall off.

Oddjob meets his demise when, inside Fort Knox, he attempts to retrieve his hat from some metal bars, which Bond then electrifies by means of an exposed cable. "That was pyrotechnics, pure pyrotechnics just like Guy Fawkes night, and very effective," says Bert.

Three hats were made in all. In 1998, one sold at auction for over £50,000. Another is owned by Sakata's daughter; the location of the third is unknown.

Another of Bert's little gimmicks was the homing device. In fact, there were two, as he explained:

> One was a tiny little thing that fitted into the heel of Bond's shoe, and the other was its bigger brother which, in the film, was planted inside Goldfinger's car. Neither actually worked, of course, but they had to look the part and have a magnetic underside. I worked on all those sorts of things; some notable, some not quite so notable!

Released in late 1964, *Goldfinger*'s success was unprecedented. The film played 24 hours a day in some cities, to meet demand. The length of the queues which formed outside cinemas had never been witnessed before. Bondmania was massive, as was Sean Connery's success.

Sadly, however, Bond's creator would not live long enough to see the third film reach cinema screens, as on August 12 Ian Fleming lost his battle with heart disease. His condition was not helped by lengthy court cases surrounding his publication of *Thunderball*.

Thunderball *and Kevin McClory*

Prior to Cubby Broccoli and Harry Saltzman's involvement, Ian Fleming took part in several attempts to bring his secret agent's exploits to the big screen. One involved a screenplay titled *James Bond of the Secret Service,* which had been a collaboration between him, screenwriter Jack Whittingham and a young producer named Kevin McClory.

The film was never made, and Fleming wrote another novel, *Thunderball.* However, many parts of the story and characters therein were identified, by McClory, as being taken from their screenplay collaboration. A lengthy lawsuit followed, resulting in McClory being awarded the film rights to the story.

McClory touted his planned production at the height of Bondmania. Anxious *not to* have their success affected by a rival film, Saltzman and Broccoli made a deal with McClory. They would act as executive producers, and he would produce. *Thunderball* became the fourth entry in the Eon series. Certain conditions were laid down in the deal with McClory, and with hindsight, the producers probably realized they were perhaps rather generous in their offer; the main point that McClory would refrain from making another version of the story for ten years. In fact, it took him almost 20 years, as in 1983 he released *Never Say Never Again* with Sean Connery reprising the role that launched his career. The film performed well, but Connery went on record as saying it was a horrible experience which saw him, with assistant director David Tomblin, effectively take over the producer role.

McClory has surfaced with other Bond projects from time to time, but each failed to materialize. In 1998 he struck a deal with Sony to produce a series of Bond adventures. It never got off the drawing board and, in a (very short) lawsuit hearing in 2000, brought by Eon and MGM to protect their ownership of the Bond character and films, McClory's case was thrown out and never again will he have cause to claim any rights concerning 007. An interesting point: Eon and MGM now own *Never Say Never Again* (as they do the re-make rights to *Casino Royale*).

Water and Ice

> The opening sequence of *Thunderball* was shot at Chateau d'Anet in France and we brought back the DB5. This time, the Aston squirts water everywhere! There were two fire engines, great big things, in front of the car, out of shot, and two big hose pipes were fed through to the back of the car. It was then about 10 degrees below zero.
>
> About 400 gallons of water squirted out with a tremendous force and as soon as the water hit the road, it froze. Within about two minutes, it was like an ice sheet. Fortunately we didn't need to re-take. I was terrified we might have to, as I'd never have cleared the road of all that ice!

In the Chateau Bond fought it out with Jacques Bouvier (played by Bob Simmons), dressed in drag as his own (supposed) widow. At one point during the fight, Bouvier throws a knife which pins Bond's sleeve to a large wall unit in the room.

> That had to be shot in reverse as no matter how competent a knife thrower we might have had, we could never have risked such a scene — not only would Sean have had something to say, the insurers would too. So I pinned Sean to the unit with the knife and used piano wire to pull it out quickly. When reversed, it looked like the knife was being thrown. Of course, it's a bit trickier than that because Sean had to film his reaction in reverse too, but some good editing and a good actor made it look perfect!

Simmons doubled for Connery in stunts throughout the series and, somewhat surprisingly, also in the famous opening gun barrel sequence. For the first three films it is Simmons that walks across the screen and fires at the camera (gun barrel). When *Thunderball* went into production using the CinemaScope technique, the sequence had to be re-filmed in a wider screen ratio and Connery was brought in.

Simmons continued on the series after Connery's departure, right through to 1981's *For Your Eyes Only* as stunt arranger.

The Jet Pack

Bond made good his escape to the DB5 from the Chateau with the use of a jump jet pack, as Bert explained:

That was a real working piece of equipment — I have the drawing of it. But it wasn't our design, we borrowed it from the American military! They do work, and have about three minutes of flight time before they peter out. They were actually designed to get men over the enemy lines — once over, they'd whip them off and go into action.

An American pilot brought one of the jet packs over to Pinewood for us — you were able to do that sort of thing when you worked for Cubby Broccoli. But he said, "I'm very sorry I can't leave it here, I have to take it away every night." We arranged it so that he brought it in every morning, and took it away again every night. Meanwhile, we were able to make an accurate copy for filming purposes. It didn't really consist of much: two cylinders and two pipes, a condenser unit and some control hand grips.

The plastering department took molds of the cylinders for me, and I did the rest. The only difference between our version and the military one was that I filled our tanks with carbon dioxide gas instead of the propulsion gases which they used — I had to because we could never have allowed Sean to use the real thing, as not only would it have been dangerous for him to maneuver, but the exhaust gases were so hot they'd have probably caused a nasty injury. Ordinarily, the pilots would have had three months training on these things; Sean had a lot less time than that!

In the event, we had Sean winched on a big crane via a couple of cables, and when he was lowered he controlled the jets of carbon dioxide gas with the levers on the hand controls, looking very much the part.

The sequence ends with Connery landing, slipping off the jet pack and popping it into the boot of the DB5 — typical James Bond!

Lightning

Bert's assignments on *Thunderball* were by no means over. His next job came with the modification of the BSA Lightning motorcycle, as used by Luciana Paluzzi in her attempts to kill Bond.

"The usual old stuff" was how Bert summed up the gadget requirements for the bike: "Rockets and that sort of thing!"

Left: The jump jet pack in *Thunderball,* seen here at Chateau Annette. *Below:* The jump jet with Bond, also at Chateau Annette.

The motorbike arrived brand new from the factory, and the effects department were advised to "run it in slowly" before it was used in the film. As Bert was the only one in the department with experience riding bikes, it was decided that he would have the task of running it in — by using it to travel to and from the studio.

I used to park the bike outside my house at night. I'd never dream of doing it nowadays, but back then you could. Every day I rode it to and from work! It looked quite mean, though, as there were two large rocket-firing tubes mounted on either side of the bike.

I was in the workshop one day and we were informed that the bike was needed up in Wardour Street, central London, for some publicity photographs. As I was the only one insured to ride it, I was landed with having to take it uptown. Now, I hated driving in London at the best of times, so wasn't too keen on the idea and was petrified of damaging the machine. Driving down the Cromwell Road (A4), I stopped at a set of red traffic lights and, out of

Bert and the BSA Lightning from *Thunderball.*

the corner of my eye, I noticed a police car stop in the second lane next to me. The passenger side window was wound down and the policeman signaled for me to pull over.

"What exactly is this, sir?" they asked, pointing to the tubes.

"Oh, they're rocket tubes," I said — immediately realizing my mistake.

It then took me a good few minutes in explaining that it was for use in a film, and of how I was off to central London. They were very nice about it, and even gave me an escort right to Wardour Street!

I'd dread to think what would happen nowadays — I'd probably be arrested before having time to explain.

Bert went on to ride the bike in a couple of scenes in the film, namely the ones filmed at Silverstone race track when Bond's DB5 is attacked. But don't worry, it wasn't *that* bike that ended up in the lake (which was in Harefield, West London); another, stand-in bike was made available for that sequence. The Luxford-modified bike is now owned by Cars of the Stars Motor Museum in Keswick.

Among the various gadgets seen in the Bahamas Q-Branch was a small underwater breathing device. It was said to contain up to four minutes of oxygen — a mini aqua lung.

It was made from two empty soda siphon cylinders — it didn't work, of course, but it looked the part. Sean used it when he was in Largo's shark pool, out in the Bahamas, and there were real live sharks in there, but separated from Sean by a sheet of Perspex. Sean was worried about the sharks getting into his part of the pool but Terence Young [the director] said, "Don't worry, the only way they'll get in is if they jump over the top like dolphins." Sean wasn't best pleased and said, "well, how the hell do you know they can't jump like dolphins?!" Well, he was quite right. So much so, in fact, that in a sequence later on when Sean had to swim through an underwater tunnel, we see him looking very surprised when a shark swims through it towards him, just before he enters. The look of surprise was a genuine one, as Sean never expected that shark to be there!

Bert's underwater breathing device, meanwhile, was attracting interest from foreign quarters, as Bert recalled:

A call came through to Pinewood from the American military, who had heard about the underwater breathing device, and Peter Lamont [who would later become production designer on the films] took it. Apparently they had heard all about our great invention and were interested in it for their armed services.

"Do you know exactly how long someone can stay underwater with one of these?" asked the American.

"Yes," replied Peter

"Well, how long?"

"For as long as you can hold your breath," exclaimed Peter.

The American gentleman was none too happy and then realized that it was only a prop; it never worked and never would!

Getting the Point

The demise of villainous Largo's henchman, Vargas (Philip Locke), was achieved rather nastily using an underwater spear gun.

Peter Lamont, production designer.

That was not an easy thing to do, because you have to have a front and rear projection. It doesn't actually penetrate, but has to look like it does. The actor had a breastplate on, obviously, to protect him. The harpoon was fired and the front section immediately retracted; the bulk of it entered the cork and metal of the breastplate and perhaps five or six inches protruded. It was all done using wires, as we had to be deadly accurate, so to say, as had the path of the harpoon strayed, it might have killed someone.

Then, in the same shot, out of the rear end came the other harpoon section — supposedly the sharp end that had traveled through the actor's body. That was done by reversing the procedure and it was filmed in one take, using two cameras.

I did have a long chat with Philip Locke before filming started, and must admit he wasn't too keen on the scene. Would you be?

Meanwhile, Largo met his end on the Disco Volante hydrofoil.

There were a few of us on the yacht, but when the two parts separated and the hydrofoil zoomed away, myself and another chap named Joe Fitt were on the back part of the yacht with 4" by 6" smoke canisters, along with oxygen and propane. When it separated, supposedly under fire, Joe and I had to start up all of the smoke and what have you. We got absolutely covered in thick black muck! If that wasn't bad enough, the

Vargos (Philip Locke) pinned to the tree in *Thunderball* thanks to Bert's harpoon rig.

winds changed during the shot and forced the smoke back into the boat. It was awful.

The final destruction of the Disco hydrofoil was done using models, and a full-size wooden re-construction, packed with explosives, which was towed out there into position. John Stears set all the explosives off. What a mess it made.

Fireworks

Bert himself made quite a few big bangs off set, as he was often called upon to prevail over firework parties.

I got on very well with Kevin McClory and, after we'd finished making the film, he called me up and said that he was hosting this big party with fireworks and what have you, would I come over to look after them? I said I'd love to and took some of my own special fireworks over — you couldn't buy this sort, as they were rather large and rather loud.

So loud were Bert's own brand fireworks that every November 5 his local police station used to brace itself for all the complaints of "shaking foundations and windows" in the area.

I'll never forget, Kevin walked into the room carrying one of these great things next to his chest, and a few inches higher his great big cigar was burning away in the corner of his mouth. We were lucky to survive that night — I think I aged 20 years. The funny thing — well, no, it wasn't funny, really — was that Kevin didn't seem overly bothered!

Harry Saltzman later made a similar request of Bert.

Harry Saltzman, or Mr. Saltzman as he always was to me, asked if I could arrange a display at his house in Chandlers, a few miles from the studio. I'd hardly call it a house — it had about ten bedrooms, four reception halls, a billiard room and lots more besides — it was quite palatial.

He was expecting about 100 people and wanted it to last about a half hour or so. Off I went and got it all organized.

In the event, it took over an hour to run through all of the display and it was marvelous. The assembled guests were delighted, and I was invited in for a drink or two. One of the first people to pop over and say hello was Roger Moore, who was, in those days, famous as "The Saint." I was introduced to Roger by Harry as "my firework man." Little did I realize in a few years I'd be working with Roger!

You'll notice that Harry Saltzman was always Mr. Saltzman and Cubby Broccoli was always Cubby — that was how it was. If you called Cubby "Mr. Broccoli," he didn't really like it. There was a big difference between them — Cubby was always warm and affectionate whereas Harry Saltzman was a bit more the stereotypical film producer, if you like. Someone once said that if Cubby gave you a cigar, instead of offering you a light, Harry Saltzman would take it off you. That rather summed him up!

There was seemingly no stopping Bond. The success of *Thunderball* eclipsed all of his previous filmic adventures. Bondmania was now at its pinnacle — and the public wanted more.

Volcanos

Sean Connery's fifth Bond adventure was *You Only Live Twice*. Definitely the most spectacular entry in the series, its production values

The mini rocket-firing cigarette in *You Only Live Twice*, made by Bert.

were immense, as was Ken Adam's giant volcano set, build on the Pinewood back lot.

In Fleming's book, archvillain Blofeld is tucked away in a Japanese castle. However, after an extensive search Japan, Ken Adam failed to find anything remotely similar. Then he had a brainstorm. In flying over some of the volcanic mountains on his recce, he noticed a great many volcanos. It was then that he wondered what it might be like to have a supposedly extinct volcano for Blofeld's rocket base.

Adam returned to Pinewood and put the idea to the producers. When asked how much it would cost to build such a set at the studio (bearing in mind no sound stage in existence anywhere in the world could house such a structure), he estimated $1 million. They told him to go ahead. His budget for this one set eclipsed the whole of *Dr. No*'s production budget!

In Adam's design, the volcano had to house a rocket firing platform; functional heliport; a closing steel curtain that covered the entire cone of the volcano and imitated the lake; a monorail; elevators; cranes; walkways and a control center. A mammoth undertaking.

> The steel curtain didn't actually exist, that's letting you into a secret. It was actually all done by Cliff Culley again, and his brilliant matte techniques. In effect, he painted all the movements of the steel door onto glass plates which were incorporated frame by frame into the film itself.

Whilst Adam designed the set, director Lewis Gilbert and writer Roald Dahl came in to plan the camera and actor's movements around it. That was vitally important; with such a huge amount of structural steel being used, it was imperative that the stress factors were calculated exactly for the movements necessary.

The Los Angeles Times published some of the construction statistics in January 1967: 200 miles of tubular steel, 700 tons of structural steel,

200 tons of plaster, 8,000 railway ties for the monorail, and 250,000 square yards of canvas to protect the set from the elements. Two hundred fifty men worked on the construction. To say it was vast would be an understatement.

Ken Adam's design for the giant volcano set in *You Only Live Twice.*

It was visible from several miles away on the main A40 road out of West London, and it dominated the studio skyline like nothing I have seen before or since.

We didn't start filming on the stage until late into 1966, after returning from Japan. My two lingering memories of it are (1) the sheer size of it and the fact that everything worked, and (2) how bloody cold it was—we'd just returned from sweltering heat in Japan to sub-zero winter temperatures!

Blofeld (Donald Pleasence) supplied a particularly menacing baddie element, after the original actor chosen for the role, Czech actor Jan Werich, was taken ill. Pleasence, whose eerie-looking features were augmented with a scar, took the honor of being the first actor to be seen on film in the role; previous incarnations had only been visible from the chest down.

Nellie

The main locations, as already mentioned, were filmed in Japan. It was there Q's appearance in the film, his second on location, came about—after Bond requested the company of "Little Nellie."

Sean Connery and Akiko Wakabayashi, *You Only Live Twice.*

I have to chuckle when I remember how Desmond talked about going on location. You see, when we were doing *Thunderball* they asked him to go out to the Bahamas as "wet weather cover." They had a set at a studio in case the heavens opened, so at least — they figured — they'd have something to fall back on and crack on with. Well, Desmond was delighted at the prospect ... but then the director, Terence Young, informed him that as Q had just arrived from London in the story, Desmond wasn't to get any sort of sun tan — so the poor old dear couldn't go out and enjoy himself! Can you imagine being flown to the Bahamas for a fortnight and not being able to sit out in the sun?

I, on the other hand, didn't have to be too concerned about catching the sun. I was out there for three months in all and came back home looking rather tanned. It was, however, a wonderful three months and we wanted for nothing. The hotels were first-class, as was the food, and Cubby was always around if we needed anything.

Well, in fact, there was one time when we did. The carnivals in Nassau were recreated especially for the film — when you're on a Bond, you can do that — and I remember well the night shooting as it got particularly cold. You can imagine the crew were all kitted out for the hot weather — and, boy, it was hot during the day. But on the first night's shooting, it really did get cold. It was mentioned to Cubby the next morning, and before anything else could be said, Cubby was off. A short time later, he returned with "007" sweatshirts for each and every member of the crew: He'd had them specially made. That's the sort of person he was— tremendously thoughtful and considerate.

I digress!

When Desmond heard he was going to Japan, he was thrilled as he'd always wanted to travel out there, and as his scenes were lined up and not just fitting in around the weather, he could get on with them straight away. But then came the news that in the scene Q was to wear shorts. Desmond hated shorts!

In later films with Roger Moore, who was quite a practical joker, Desmond would often walk on set only to hear the director and Roger saying "Yes, Q should be in shorts for this scene." It used to drive him crazy.

However, Desmond — plus shorts— arrived in Japan and along with him came "Little Nellie."

Not an elderly aunt as one might initially suppose, but rather an autogyro. A radio trailer for the film perhaps summed it up best:

High above an extinct Japanese volcano.
Four heavily armored black helicopters spin through the sky.

Their target —
one man in a flying
arsenal, that fits in
two alligator suit-
cases.

The odds, four to
one.

They haven't got
a chance.

"Little Nellie" was
designed and built by
Wing Commander Ken
Wallis, and was one of three military type WA-116s built in 1962.
The Wallis autogyros still, to this
day, hold most of the official
World Records for speed, time to
climb, altitude, range and dura-
tion.

While shaving one morn-
ing, Ken Adam was listening to
a radio interview in which Wallis was talking about his autogyros and how, given the chance,
he would love to pit them
against helicopters. The rest, as
they say, is history.

A most irate Q arrives in
Japan, annoyed at having to
drop everything at a moments
notice with four (not two as the
advert said) large suitcases.

Top: Little Nellie and the camera helicopter. *Bottom:* Little Nellie airborne.

Of course, Nellie could never
have been contained in those
cases like that, and built up in a matter of minutes; but that's the magic
of film. Sean then flew it, or rather Wing Commander Wallis did, over
the Japanese countryside with ruddy big rockets that we fitted on it.
They were three and a half foot long. John Stears and I tested one on the
Pinewood back lot and we aimed it over Black Park, just to see what
would happen. It did a full circle, though, and turned back. It landed

Preparing Little Nellie.

about 20 foot from us.

Dear Ken [Wallis] didn't really anticipate the weight load of these large rockets, plus smaller clusters on the side and the machine guns, aerial mines, etc. that I fitted on the autogyro. The rockets were live, in the respect of them having a live shot gun cartridge and black powder in the tip. They were quite lethal, really. Ken was very patient though, and rehearsed time after time in this tiny little aircraft. It all worked brilliantly in the end, apart from him getting bloody cold flying it in short sleeves.

Quite honestly, that was the most enjoyable location that I've ever been on, it really was great fun with Ken, Desmond and Sean; for three months. I'll forever remember the little schoolgirls over there saying that I was the Devil too! You see, I had reddish hair in those days, and that was regarded as being Satan's hair, and it was very rare in Japan. It really was quite funny.

Smoking!

While in Japan, Bert also helped furnish their version of Q-Branch. The rocket cigarette, as demonstrated by Tiger Tanaka, did actually work:

Sean Connery and Desmond Llewelyn.

It was a little rocket with a tiny touch fuse on it, planted inside a cigarette. When someone lit the cigarette, it quickly burnt down to the fuse, and out shot the rocket. It did work (although it didn't bang!). But we didn't let the actors use it: Some of them had trouble learning lines, let alone anything else.

Bert also made the throwing stars and several of the other weapons used in the Ninja school, along with many of the swords as used in the fight sequences. They now fetch an absolute fortune at auction.

Top and bottom: The ninja training school in *You Only Live Twice.*

With the next film, a new James Bond was introduced in the shape of Australian model George Lazenby. The gadgets and gimmicks were not too evident, and as such Bert's work was confined to "the usual little bits and pieces" associated with incidental effects, as on *Dr. No.*

The Other Bond

I suppose I should really make mention of another Bond film I was involved with at this time too. It wasn't an "official" 007 adventure, but a quite terrible spoof called *Casino Royale.*

It actually shot around most of the studios in London: Pinewood, Shepperton, Elstree … it was everywhere. Charles K. Feldman was the producer, as he had acquired the film rights some years earlier. Ian Fleming had sold those early on, and only the rights to that film.

Casino Royale was manic. We had half a dozen directors and guest stars virtually popping in every other day. Feldman used to grab any personality who was in London and give them a cameo. It was a star-studded picture, but because the script kept changing and there were so many directors, it didn't really work.

The star was, of course, David Niven, who played an aging Sir James Bond. I have to admit that David Niven was a bit of a childhood hero of mine, and I very much enjoyed meeting him, albeit briefly.

My stint on the film was, like so many other, on what I call itsy-bitsy work. During one of the big fight sequences, towards the film's finale, they wanted colored smoke bursts drifting in the air; so the "aerial bursts" were all mine. I didn't get involved in any of the big explosions such as where John Huston was "blown up" as they were in another studio. But it was quite an experience all the same and was around Pinewood for the best part of a year.

Connery Departs

Back in the Eon fold, George Lazenby's one and only Bond film, *On Her Majesty's Secret Service* was, in comparison to the early films, a box office disappointment. Editor cum second unit director Peter Hunt took the reins, and in doing so made one of the best (and truest to Fleming) films in the series.

The supporting cast included Diana Rigg and Telly Savalas. John Barry composed some of his finest film music ever.

The "star" of the film, Lazenby, made a fatal mistake. He thought the Bond bandwagon was running out of steam and was advised to make one film, get out and capitalize on his newfound stardom. He really did think he was a star, and so acted like one — alienating the producers and director in the process. Before shooting was over, Lazenby made it clear that he wouldn't be doing another Bond. The publicity, therefore, was centered on anything and anyone except Lazenby, who himself rolled up to the premiere with a bushy beard, much to the chagrin of Cubby Broccoli. He later admitted to regretting his actions as his career plummeted to supporting roles and spoof comedies.

Critically the film was successful, but commercially it took several years to turn a profit.

Connery Returns

United Artists and Eon Productions were adamant that if Bond was to survive, they needed Connery back. Talks took place to no avail, until UA's David Picker personally flew out to meet with Connery. A deal was hatched that made the headlines: a mammoth $1 million fee plus substantially more should the schedule run over, plus a stake in profits, plus a green-light on any other two projects Connery wanted to make. He made only one film under the deal, *The Offence* (which is probably one of the least commercial films he has made), but in it delivers a brilliant performance as a detective on the verge of a mental breakdown. Directed by Sidney Lumet, it co-starred Trevor Howard and Ian Bannen.

Connery's $1 million *Diamonds Are Forever* fee was donated to the charity which he founded, the Scottish International Education Trust.

With Connery's return came a slight increase in the use of gimmicks. Bert's involvement was sought in the pre-title sequence, as he explained:

> Bond enters Blofeld's lab and is seeking revenge for the murder of his wife in the previous film. There, they come face to face and Blofeld is overpowered, strapped to a table and plunged into this bubbling goo. In fact, I used mashed potatoes mixed with cocoa. We had hundreds of these bags of mashed potato powder, and I remember they stamped "not fit for human consumption" on the side, so as the crew wouldn't pinch it. Mind you, me and the wife enjoyed a couple of 'em — didn't do us any harm.

Actors!

Bert took a break on the next film, Roger Moore's first, *Live and Let Die*, but was soon drafted for Moore's second, *The Man with the Golden Gun*, after a little mishap on set.

> Ah, yes. Don't get me wrong, I have the utmost respect for actors, but also know that they're not all technical experts either, and don't always fully appreciate what might go into to making something. Well, a lighter company called Colibri made the actual golden gun, which came together by assembling a cigarette case, lighter, cufflink and pen. It was gorgeous, and was all diamond cut. But someone made the mistake of giving it to an actor — I don't know who, or how — to play around with and it was dropped, smashing into tiny pieces.
>
> A frantic art director came running into my workshop and said, "they've busted the gun!" and he asked me if I could make another one.

I asked how long, and he said, "You've got a little more than tomorrow." I said I'd need a little more than two weeks, at least.

I got together with a colleague of mine, Curly Currs, who was a gunsmith, and we set about making another one, out of more durable brass. The thing was, we knew that it then had to go over to Ireland to be diamond cut, as that was the only place it was done, and that would add days.

The golden gun from *The Man with the Golden Gun.*

The film schedule was re-arranged, and we worked around the clock. We made it in just over a week, and flew it to Ireland. It was on stage within a fortnight of the "incident." Of course, we all realized that Colibri's mistake was in making only one of the guns; really, they should have had a standby one too, but we all live and learn.

The *Golden Gun* plot involved solar energy, and in particular a device called the solex agitator, which was the key component in planned cheap solar energy production. It was stolen by Francisco Scaramanga, a.k.a. the man with the golden gun, played by Christopher Lee — who had uses other than saving the world's energy crisis in mind. It was left to Bond to recover it.

Although terribly valuable and complicated in the film, the agitator was anything but, as Bert explained:

I was given a sketch, and the idea. The thing was about three inches by six inches and had to look "electronic"

The solex agitator which Bert made for *The Man with the Golden Gun* (close up).

Opposite, top: Blofeld lands in the goo, the mashed potato and cocoa powder mixture Bert concocted for the pre-title sequence in *Diamonds Are Forever.* **Bottom:** Bond washes down the "man in the goo."

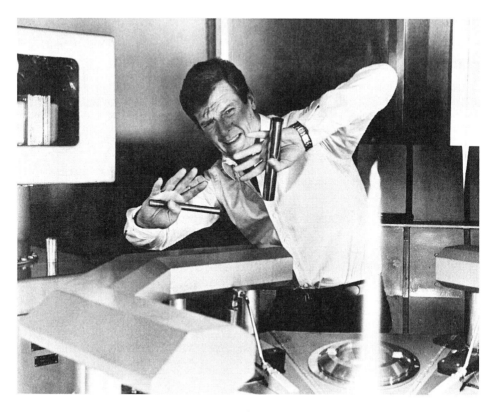

Roger Moore as 007 tries to retrieve the solex in the *The Man with the Golden Gun.*

The solex agitator, *The Man with the Golden Gun.*

in some way. I molded, in a clear plastic rectangle, a group of resistors, capacitors and coils. It looked like a glorified paperweight. Yet it did the trick. It's absolutely useless in real life, though.

It was often the case that gadgets and gimmicks would only appear in a film for perhaps 10 or 20 seconds in all, but that was not to diminish its importance or the amount of money the producers would spend.

We might have spent something like £20,000 on a sequence involving a gadget that would appear on screen for a relatively short time, and that was over 20 years ago, but Cubby Broccoli never skimped when it came to films. He would say, "If that's what it costs, so be it." That was his attitude, and that was such a wonderful thing to have in a producer. Nowadays effects men have to budget for every single item, before filming starts, and that's very difficult.

Prankster

With the new Bond came a wicked sense of humor. Roger Moore was renowned for practical jokes and windups, and took advantage of any weaknesses he could spot in a colleague's armor. With Desmond Llewelyn, Moore had some of his greatest fun.

Poor Desmond wasn't tremendously good at remembering his lines, and you must remember that he did have a lot of technical stuff to spout at times. He used to pace the corridors at the studio frantically committing it to memory.

I remember Roger used to get into cahoots with the director and script girl, and they'd re-write pages of Desmond's dialogue as some of the worst gobbledey-gook you'd ever seen. The director would then hand it to Desmond and say, "Sorry, old boy, the script has changed for this afternoon."

So off went Desmond, through his lunch break, committing this new stuff to memory. Only when he turned up on set Roger would be creasing himself with laughter, and the penny dropped.

From time to time Desmond would have prompt cards, or idiot boards as he called them, just to remind him of the script. During one scene of close-ups on Desmond, Roger kindly suggested that he'd hold the boards. One by one he pulled them back as Desmond progressed through the dialogue and then, all of a sudden, there would be one saying "Bollocks." Needless to say, it brought the house down.

I was involved in a few of Roger's films in small ways, doing odds and sods, but nothing wildly exciting as the bigger the films got, the bigger their own particular departments got, including effects. So they didn't really need little me that much. But it was great fun with him.

Bert, Eunice Gayson and Gareth Owen at the Desmond Llewelyn tree planting, Pinewood Studios, May 2000. (Robin Harbour.)

Q

Desmond tragically died in a car crash just before Christmas 1999, a few days after penning the Foreword to this book. Ironically, I had been with him only a few weeks earlier celebrating the launch of his biography, *Q*. In later years Desmond had become something of a super-star through his role in the films, though he remained unchanged and as friendly as ever — but with seemingly more energy than ever too.

Following the tremendous success of *Goldeneye* (1995) and *Tomorrow Never Dies* (1997), Desmond Llewelyn was constantly out-and-about promoting Bond, guesting at functions or making appearances on TV and in films. He had a particular enthusiasm for helping student filmmakers and, despite not being paid other than his expenses, would travel far and wide to appear in their films, helping them on their way. His travels on the Bond promotional trail were extensive: from Los Angeles and New York, to Holland and Spain, back to Los Angeles then onto the U.K., then off to Paris

... all in a few weeks. When asked how he managed to maintain such a grueling work schedule in his eighties, Llewelyn smiled and said:

> I get picked up outside my front door in a limousine. At the airport I'm whisked through the VIP lounge and into a first-class seat on the plane. At the other end I'm picked up by a limousine and taken to a top-class hotel suite which dwarfs my own house. There all my meals and drinks are paid for and I want for nothing. In return, I have to give a little talk on Bond which I could do in my sleep. You call that hard work?

Bert recalls,

> The last time I met up with Roger Moore was in March 2000 at the memorial service for Desmond in London. There he spoke very affectionately of Desmond and said, "Whilst some people say the Bond films will never be the same with Q, I will say the Bond films will never be the same without Desmond Llewelyn." How I echo those words.
>
> I was very privileged to be invited to Pinewood Studios in May to plant a tree in memory of my dear old friend Desmond. Eunice Gayson joined me along with representatives from Eon Productions and many friends and colleagues. It was a particularly moving afternoon and one I was proud to be involved with.
>
> I always look back on the Bond films and the folks on them with great affection and pride, particularly the first few with Sean; they still stand up so well when shown on TV today. Each new film in the series now, with Pierce Brosnan, still brings the excitement we all encountered in the early days, and they still deliver what the public wants: great stunts, effects and action, beautiful girls, exotic locations and wonderful villains. There are, of course, many imitators of the films: from James Coburn's Derek Flint to Mike Myers' Austin Powers. But one thing is for sure, you can never beat the real thing.
>
> Nowadays the effects on Bond are handled by a talented bunch of guys under the supervision of Chris Corbould, who I've known since he was knee-high, and my old chum John Richardson, who worked miracles with his miniatures in the last two pictures. With the public's appetite for Bond still so great, and with such a talented team making each bigger and better than the last, I know for sure that the films will be around for quite a few more years to come, and I look forward to them. That's a very satisfying thought!
>
> As they say at the end of each film, "James Bond Will Return."

SCENE FOUR

Just a Jobbing Technician

Whilst Pinewood was kept busy with the annual or (later) biannual visits from James Bond, it also played host to scores of many other films: comedies, dramas, action, horror and so forth. Needless to say, most involved the odd gimmick or two, and most called upon the white-coated gentlemen in the studio's workshops. The majority of work was pretty run-of-the-mill, but there were the odd exceptions. In his field, Bert's reputation was second to none, but in the name of his art he gained himself something of a dubious reputation in his local shopping center too.

I did have to do some unusual things, such as being commissioned to make a giant pair of knickers for a cow — a real cow. It was quite a specific order: white with big red dots, or red with big white dots. So off I trotted to Suitors department store in Uxbridge, where I was met with raised eyebrows from the staff. I had a terrible name there, I tell you. I was always there asking for strange things, but they were very nice about it as I spent a lot of money.

For this assignment, I went to the upholstery department and requested the fabric. When asked how much I wanted, I sort of held my arms out, as wide as my shoulders. But the assistant wanted me to be more specific, and asked what I wanted it for. So, I told her: "Enough to make a pair of knickers for a cow." You can imagine the look I got.

"And what size is your good lady?" came the much-thought-about response.

"They're not for my lady, they're for a real cow."

It took some explaining, but I got there in the end. I did some

70

bloody silly things, but that was part of my job: It wasn't just blowing up cars, and setting fire to buildings, of which I did do a lot admittedly. There was a lot more to it like this; which, as you might appreciate, isn't something I talk about a great deal about.

It wasn't just Bert who was making a somewhat notorious name for himself at the local shops (of which there will be more later), but his colleagues too.

I'll always remember my dear friend Jimmy Snow being asked to make a string of sausages for a production. They had to be quite lightweight as they were to be thrown around. Simple enough? Hmmm.

You must remember that this was 30 years ago or more, and attitudes were a bit more conservative than nowadays as regards certain things. So when Jimmy went into Boots the chemist and asked for a complete box of tampons, it took a lot of doing. It was a woman that served him too, of course.

"Eh?" she said.

"A complete box of tampons please."

"Are you sure?"

"Oh yes," enthused Jimmy.

Poor little Jimmy, and he was only small, had to carry this great big box which must have been two foot by one foot by one and a half foot, with stickers all over it, out of Boots and all the way back to the studio. Once back, he took a half gallon of latex, put it in a bucket with a bit of pink dye and then dipped them all in. Out came a string of lightweight sausages!

That was us, though. We did things you wouldn't have thought of — we'd improvise and innovate. It was great fun too.

In Traction

Along with *Carry On* films, of which more later, producer Peter Rogers and director Gerald Thomas made a great many others — mainly comedies — at Pinewood. Among them was the 1962 production *The Iron Maiden* starring Michael Craig, Cecil Parker, Alan Hale, Jr., Lionel Jeffries and Noel Purcell — one of Bert's favorite pictures.

It was a lovely film to work on. We had to recreate the Iron Maiden herself out of wood; "her" being a gigantic steam traction engine.

For one scene, we needed the Maiden to end up in a big ditch. Four tons of Iron Maiden could not have been dumped down the ditch very easily, nut more importantly it would have taken eight tons of lifting equipment to get it out again — on each take.

Therefore the carpenters department built the body out of wood, about 15 people worked on that, and I had to do the rest of the functional bits: the various wheels, levers, the smoke coming out of the puff-puff. In effect, I brought the machine to life, although it was all false.

A lot was filmed opposite Iver Village Church in the gardens; we must have been there for three weeks in all. The film was all about a steam engine race, and how one of the entrants sabotaged the Maiden's chances of winning by digging a ditch there, covering it with grass and leaving it for the engine to fall into.

Alan Hale was brilliant, as he had to drive the Maiden and was very proficient in it too; and he didn't mind getting dirty either. You'd never notice the difference between the real thing and "our" version. I was very proud of that.

Fore!

Shortly after completing *The Iron Maiden*, Bert returned to the Eon fold for their only non–Bond film, *Call Me Bwana* (1963), again with Lionel Jeffries ... amongst others.

That was ever such a funny film, and I really enjoyed working with Bob Hope in the supposedly jungle set comedy. In fact, it was all filmed around Pinewood with potted palm trees brought in.

We had a little elephant on the film, along with other animals shipped in for effect, and it was attracted to a certain scent you see. A lady's scent, perfume. If you watch the film, you'll see it pop its trunk through a window and kiss Bob — because I sprayed some scent on him. Nobody realized how we did it until about halfway through the film! It worked every time.

Of the other animals brought in there were two giraffes which were taken to the location at Gerrards Cross Golf Club a couple of miles from the studio. They made an interesting sight riding in the back of large open-top trucks.

Over the weekend it was agreed that the giraffes could stay on an enclosed part of the course and have someone keeping an eye on them. However, this was all unbeknownst to the Club Captain's wife. It so happened that their house backed on to the course and on the Sunday afternoon, the Captain's wife was attending to her roses when she felt her straw hat moving. She looked up to see a giraffe tucking in to it. She fainted and came to in the local hospital, not quite knowing what had happened.

Meanwhile, another effect that John Stears and I worked on was in rigging a Jeep to fall to pieces. No easy task. On a cue, all of the wheels had to fall off, along with the doors, and the whole thing had to crash to the floor, but it had to be repeatable too, for retakes.

It was all achieved with cables and levers and rigged such that cables were holding the wheels in place, and one pull on the lever triggered the lot to fall off. A fairly complicated set-up, using all my engineering skills; it was all manual too, no electronics. Thankfully, it worked on take one.

Bogarde

A brief stint followed on *Doctor in Distress* with the producer-director team of Betty Box and Ralph Thomas, and with Rank's biggest star of the day in the lead once again. Dirk Bogarde had already starred in the first two films of the series (*Doctor in the House* and *Doctor at Sea*) before breaking free from Dr Simon Sparrow to pursue other, more serious roles. However, when the third installment, *Doctor in Trouble* (with Leslie Phillips and Michael Craig), proved rather successful, Bogarde suggested he wouldn't mind coming back for another *Doctor* film. *Distress* became the fourth in the series, and Bogarde's last.

Dirk was fun. He was a very big star too. In fact, he was probably the only British star of the day who could "open" a film on his own.

The *Doctor*

Doctor in the House. Jack Swinburne, Ralph Thomas, Gerald Thomas, Betty Box and Muriel Box. (Gareth Owen Collection.)

films were wonderful comedy, but I remember Dirk saying he didn't want to do it for the rest of his life, he wanted to tackle dramatic stories too. One such dramatic film he starred in was *The Wind Cannot Read*. It had an unfortunate alternative title around the studio though: *The Illiterate Fart*. In it, Dirk played a flying officer who falls in love with a Japanese language instructor in World War II Burma.

I remember hearing a lovely story about that film. Not many knew this, but Dirk actually had a false tooth at the front of his top set. He'd wear it all the time, apart from when he took it out to go to bed, but even then he kept it nearby on his bed-side table.

On location, Dirk was having terrible trouble in sleeping at night. So much so, he looked quite awful as the days went by. The director, Ralph Thomas, was becoming rather concerned and suggested Dirk might take a sleeping pill to help him get off to sleep at night. Dirk wasn't at all keen on that idea.

However, Ralph left a couple of pills in Dirk's room on the bedside table and told him to take one if he couldn't get to sleep after an hour or so.

At three in the morning, Ralph was woken with a start. There was frantic knocking on his room door. He opened it to be greeted by a gaunt-looking Dirk Bogarde.

When Ralph inquired what the matter was, Dirk told him that he was having trouble getting off to sleep so decided to try one of the pills. A few hours later he woke up, and visited the loo. On returning to bed he noticed that the two pills were still there. Then, it dawned on him. He'd actually swallowed his false tooth.

If that wasn't bad enough, later that morning the schedule called for a number of quite specific closeups on Dirk. But how could they do it with him missing his tooth? Panic set in.

To cut a long story short, half a dozen bottles of castor oil were rounded up, and a bottle of disinfectant. Need I say more than the closeups were filmed, tooth and all?

Dirk Bogarde appeared in 30 or so films for the Rank Organisation, his last being *The Singer Not the Song* with John Mills. He went on to great acclaim in films such as *Victim* (which challenged the laws on homosexuality in Britain), *Death in Venice* and, finally, *Daddy Nastolgie* in 1990. He was knighted in 1992 and died in 1999.

Disney and Syn

It wasn't long before Bert rekindled his associations from his first film *The Horse Without a Head*, as with both Disney and Patrick McGoohan

he was engaged on *Dr. Syn Alias the Scarecrow*. A re-working of the 1937
Dr. Syn starring George Arliss, itself based on Russell Thorndike's novel
Christopher Syn, the film centered around the Vicar of Dymchurch's alter
ego of a smuggler (a.k.a. The Scarecrow), portrayed here as something of
a Robin Hood figure. Patrick McGoohan played the titular roles, with support from George Cole, Tony Britton, Kay Walsh and Geoffrey Keen.

> Patrick and I never really hit it off, I must admit. We never disagreed,
> and he was a lovely man don't get me wrong, but we just didn't get
> along too well. He was an intensely private person, with a very straight-
> laced personality and rarely smiled. He kept himself very much to him-
> self and wasn't the sort who would strike up a conversation to pass away
> the time between set-ups, as many of other actors I've worked with
> would have. So it was a bit of a strange film to work on in that respect.
> Jimmy Ackland Snow and I worked on all manner of bits and pieces.
> We weren't on set all the time, only when we were called as I was still
> (like Jimmy) under contract with Pinewood, not the film company.
> We did anything and everything from fires to stuffing straw up peo-
> ple's backs. I would say out of the six-week shoot we were on for four
> or five days.

A Little Wisdom

Unquestionably, one of Rank's biggest little stars was Norman Wisdom.

The 5 foot, 4¾ inch funny man made a name for himself in the variety halls after a turbulent childhood: When Wisdom was just nine years
of age, his mother left him and his brother with their father who beat
them, disappeared for weeks on end and showed them little, if any, love.
After being passed from pillar to post and living rough for a time, he was
persuaded to join the Army. There he excelled as a musician, and was fed
regularly and clothed — things which he had never been able to take for
granted before.

One night Norman started shadow boxing in the barracks, and when
he allowed the shadow to hit him back, the whole barracks were in hysterics. From then, young Norman knew it was comedy for him.

His first professional engagement saw him on the same bill as Laurel
and Hardy; his comic genius was immediately recognized and he was
besieged by agents.

Many stage and TV appearances followed until, in 1952, during the
successful run of *Paris to Piccadilly* at London's Prince of Wales Theatre,

Desmond Llewelyn and Sir Norman Wisdom. (Gareth Owen Collection.)

his agent Billy Marsh dashed in, saying the Rank Organisation had offered Norman a seven-picture contract.

The first film was never made after Norman was auditioned by director Ronald Neame with Petula Clark in what was a "serious piece." However, keen to exploit the comic potential of their new contractee, Rank commissioned a script especially for Norman. It was *Trouble in Store*, directed by John Paddy Carstairs, and an amazing hit.

It was a fantastic success, but up until the time it was previewed, nobody thought it would be. In truth, the Rank Organisation became nervous about their signing, especially after the first film under the contract was never made.

Norman told me that they ran a preview in a cinema in North London. When he arrived, all of the "gray suits" were there and greeted him rather curtly with "Good evening, Mr. Wisdom" and "We hope you're successful" and then "Best of luck with it, Mr. Wisdom." All very formal. When the film started, Norman sat in his seat watching the audience's reaction. Mercifully, they loved the film.

On the way out, the same "gray suits" were there to greet Norman. This time it was quite different:

"Oh, dear Norman, we knew it would be a success."

"Marvelous work, Norman, we always had faith in you."

You know the stuff. Norman says he calls it "the bullshit of show business." Unfortunately, there is a lot of it in our industry.

From his first film, the little genius climbed the success ladder at a tremendous pace. An annual Wisdom film became part of the diary.

Wisdom was notorious for involving himself in every single aspect of his films, particularly the stunts.

A Stitch in Time was definitely one of Norman's best films, and I know he agrees with that. I got on tremendously well with Norman; who doesn't? A lot of people underrate him as just being a fall-about clown. That's wrong. He's a very accomplished actor, and a bloody good one too—I soon found that out.

My only complaint would be that he sometimes petrified me with the stunts. He's only about 5'4" and quite a slim bloke, and so when I heard they were going to have him — in bandages—crash through a wall, onto the top of an ambulance, speed away and then end up flying back into a ward, I was horrified. They did, in fact, decide to do it with a stuntman, but he broke his leg and Norman stepped in.

The bandages served as great padding, and when he landed on the ambulance roof, we rigged a turntable-type thing so that he could spin around (whilst being secured to the roof) and wires to stop him falling off the side. He did it all though, and I took my hat off to him.

Just as all of the stunts were played for real, so were all of the other scenes:

There is a sequence where Norman is playing the trombone when a kiddie throws an ice cream in the end. Norman stops playing, then blows the mouthpiece as hard as he can. With it, the ice cream flies out again. There was no trickery in it. Granted it may have taken a couple of takes, but it was done for real.

Arise Sir Norman

Bert's admiration for Norman Wisdom could best be described as mixed. Yes, he has tremendous respect for the performer and actor, but at the same time is all too aware of the precarious position in which Norman placed himself, and the crew whose livelihood depended on him. The insurers were never really happy either, but that wasn't a consideration for Norman.

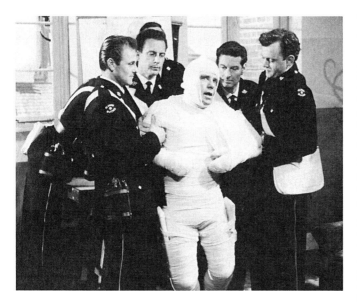

From *A Stitch in Time*: Sir Norman Wisdom is plastered! (Gareth Owen Collection.)

When I say that we rigged a turntable on the roof of the ambulance, well, yes we did but it wasn't quite as simple as Norman just lying on it; when Norman fell he had to secure himself to the clasp, otherwise he'd have flown off. That was the tricky bit — making it all look real, whilst Norman had time to protect himself properly. So as to not slow down the action when Norman fiddled around a bit in securing himself, we slowed the cameras down for that part of the scene. They rehearsed for ages, and very scientifically, resulting in it all working brilliantly. That's a perfect example of how all the departments work together in achieving the effect. We had stunts, wardrobe (with padding), the cameraman and little me: a real team effort.

A Stitch in Time actually knocked Sean Connery's second Bond outing *From Russia With Love* off the box-office top spot. There was no ill feeling between the stars, however, as they often enjoyed a round of golf together on courses near the studio.

Bert worked with Norman again the following year on *The Early Bird*. The first ten minutes of the film is played without a word of dialogue, and the first glimpse we catch of Norman — once again playing downtrodden Norman Pitken and in this incarnation, a milkman — is of him in bed, being woken up by an elaborate Heath Robinson alarm system, courtesy of Bert.

That was fun in the way it all worked. One thing would knock onto another and another, and so forth. It became like a domino effect of gimmicks to wake Norman and get him out of bed. I didn't do much

Left: Sir Norman Wisdom, admiring the view. *Right:* Sir Norman Wisdom, grabbing a bite.

else on the film after that, just a few odds and sods, but it was nice to work with Norman again and, thankfully, in less precarious circumstances.

Wisdom made 13 films in total at Pinewood between 1953 and 1966. His stage and small screen appearances were many and notable in the post–Pinewood days.

He did a marvelous TV film for the BBC in the 1980s with director Stephen Frears, called *Going Gently.* In it, Norman played a terminally ill cancer patient — along with fellow patient Fulton Mackay, and Judi Dench as the nurse. It brought to the fore his wonderful ability to play comedy and pathos almost hand in hand. However, Stephen Frears was a little unsure initially.

Norman was having lunch at the BBC with the producer, Innes Lloyd, and Stephen asked him if he realized that this was a serious piece of drama and not a slapstick comedy. Norman said he knew, but couldn't they at least have a bit of fun with say him stepping into a bed pan, pulling the sheets off the bed and.... With that, Stephen stood up and said he wanted to see Norman in his office.

They went up to his office, but before Frears started on about how it wasn't a comedy again, Norman raised his voice to him and said how dare he treat him like this; didn't he know he (Norman) could get work anywhere he wanted? He could pack theaters out, his films were still running all over the world and he didn't need to work, let alone be treated like he didn't know what he was talking about. Frears was dumbstruck, he didn't know what to say — and Norman looked pretty angry!

Norman then smiled and asked, "How about that for acting then?"

To this day, Norman remains a firm favorite with family audiences all over the world, and even with Royal families. In January 2000 he was knighted by Queen Elizabeth for services to show business, having been described as both the Queen and Queen Mother's favorite comedian. But despite being an octogenarian, the lovable comedian couldn't resist his little trademark trip as he walked away from the Queen, to the amusement of all in the Grand Ballroom at Buckingham Palace.

SCENE FIVE

Carry On!

Just as Bert Luxford had become involved and, to a point, synonymous with the Bond films, he soon rolled up his sleeves and joined the gang on the *Carry On* films, thereby insuring his working on Britain's two most successful film series.

The brainchild of producer Peter Rogers, the series came to life in 1958 with *Carry On Sergeant*. It was based on a treatment of R. F. Delderfield's *The Bull Boys*, and in noting the potential of the storyline, Rogers brought in his contract scriptwriter Norman Hudis to look over the treatment and replace the ballet dancer leads of the original story with a newly married couple, desperately trying to consummate their union.

Rogers had already carved a successful career as a film screenwriter and producer before the *Carry On*s came along. He started out as a writer with J. Arthur Rank's Religious Films before then deciding to pursue a career in journalism. However a meeting with producer Sydney Box, who then ran the Gainsborough Studio, led to Rogers being asked about scenarios for Box's production *Holiday Camp*. It was the first of many collaborations. At Gainsborough, Rogers met and married Sydney's sister, Betty, who went on to be the most prolific female film producer in the business. Rogers himself soon progressed through the ranks and in 1953 he produced his first film, *You Know What Sailors Are*, directed by Ken Annakin.

In 1956, he offered editor Gerald Thomas (brother of director Ralph) his chance of directing a children's feature, *Circus Friends*. The film attracted good notices and so was born a partnership that spanned almost

The *Carry On* Men: Director Gerald Thomas and producer Peter Rogers.
(Gareth Owen Collection.)

40 years and included many non–*Carry On* films, one of which was *Time-lock* with a pre–Bond Sean Connery.

The success of *Carry On Sergeant*, however, insured the duo would follow up with another; this time it was *Nurse*. It launched *Carry On* fever.

Carry On Teacher was hastily followed with *Constable*, *Regardless*, *Cabby* and *Jack* and a regular team was established both in front and behind the camera. The acting regulars (Sid James, Kenneth Williams, Charles Hawtrey, Kenneth Connor, Joan Sims, Barbara Windsor and Hattie Jacques) were later joined by the likes of Jim Dale, Bernard Bresslaw, Terry Scott and Peter Butterworth.

The films were famed for coming in on schedule and on budget despite having only five- or six-week schedules, and rarely using more than one camera.

I Spy

Ironically, Bert's first *Carry On* was none other than the spoof of the Bond films, *Spying* (1964).

THEY'RE AT IT AGAIN-OOOH!

KENNETH
WILLIAMS
BARBARA
WINDSOR
BERNARD
CRIBBINS
CHARLES
HAWTREY
ERIC
BARKER
DILYS
LAYE

PETER
ROGERS

CARRY ON SPYING

Carry On Spying. The poster that upset 007's producers.

The *Carry Ons* were very different from the Bond films. Yes, of course, they were smaller budgets and tighter schedules, but there was always a tremendously enjoyable, fun and friendly atmosphere on set. There was [that atmosphere] Bond, but I felt a bit more pressured with 007 as each became bigger and more demanding. *Carry On* was like "playtime" in a way, Peter Rogers and Gerry Thomas (the director) had created a marvelous formula with a fantastic group of actors. I grew to love them all.

To my way of thinking, the films were based very much on the old saucy seaside postcard humor. It didn't appeal to everyone, I know, and they weren't forced to watch the films — but usually had a moan all the same — but the humor did appeal to a heck of a lot of people, and it still does. It's harmless fun, so why not?

For *Spying*, my instructions were quite simply. Get a gun with an upturned barrel. It sounds easy, but you try it. I started playing around with blank firers to see if I could bend the barrel, but it wasn't any good. So I decided I'd make the whole damn thing myself, and I did. Of course, it didn't really work, I wouldn't dare give an actor a gun that did, but it was effective for our purposes. It went on to feature in the film's poster, sending up the *From Russia with Love* poster, and a lawsuit followed from the Bond producers, who were unhappy about it (my gun was used in the poster artwork!). Thankfully it was all resolved.

Bilko in Britain

In 1967, Bert's involvement in the series increased dramatically with *Carry On Follow That Camel.*

That was the one with Phil Silvers, and it was the first time I'd met him. He was a very nice chap actually, and I remember he'd had a bit of an

Carry On … Follow That Camel: Bert leaning up against "Fort 69."

upset in his family life back in America before coming over for the film, but he never let that show. He wasn't a bad card player either — you see, I'm letting you into a secret there, as usually Charlie Hawtrey, Frank George and I would sit in the back of the wagon between scenes and play cards, and on *Camel*, Phil used to sit in with us. Charlie used to win most of the time, but Phil gave him a run for his money.

I always found Phil to be totally calm, cool and collected; totally the opposite to his Bilko character.

Work called, however, and out on location in Camber Sands, Surrey, Gerry said that he wanted a trench about ten feet long, three feet deep and full of gunge around the French Foreign Legion Fort.

The prop men dug the trench, and Frank George and I had to concoct the "gunge." We ended up going down the road to a hardware shop, bought 50 great big packets of polycell and mixed it with water and all sorts of other rubbish — earth, sand and so on — and sprinkled earth over the top. You'd never have known the trench was there … until the actors ended up in it. Oh the glamour of it all.

Bert took charge of all of the firearms and swords, and the many pyrotechnics involved in the final siege of the Fort. He also had to help find a solution to a rather novel problem:

Still on Camber Sands, Gerry said he was going to do the scenes involving the camel which involved it walking across the sand, with Phil Silvers and some of the other characters.

Just as they started to turn-over it started snowing — a real old downpour, actually. We thought it would be the end of the day's shoot, but just then, Gerry turned to his director of photography [Alan Hume] and said, "Put a yellow filter on, Alan, and we'll call it a sandstorm." They did, and it bloody well worked too, and is in the film. Such was Gerry's genius.

Carry On ... Follow That Camel. Sheena leads Phil Silvers, Kenneth Williams, Jim Dale, Charles Hawtrey, Bernard Bresslaw, Peter Butterworth and Anita Harris. (Gareth Owen Collection.)

Then we realized we had a problem with the camel. It wouldn't walk on the sand. You see, it came from a zoo and had been so used to the hard standing that sand must have seemed a very strange surface.

Would you believe we had to lay down emergency airplane runway strips under the sand so as to create the illusion, for the camel, of it being a hard surface? We managed to get away with it too.

It was a great location, and a wonderfully funny time, and I remember that at night we used to go over to a place, a pub actually, called The Green Shutters, which is still there. It only opened at night, never during the day, but dear Charles always used to come over and he'd say "Can we go for a pint yet?" It was always too early, of course, but I think the thought of that lovely, cool pint kept us going. It wasn't that we were drunkards by any means, it was more of a social thing, but was such a pleasant part of the day that we all really looked forward to it.

I miss Charles, as I do the others, but was particularly saddened at the circumstances surrounding his death, and the way the media reported it. It wasn't very nice, I know, but the press made it seem much worse when they wrote about his drinking and various "affairs" with young men. I'll always remember him as a damn nice bloke, and that's what's most important.

Follow That Camel, the second in the series financed by the Rank Organisation, was a runaway success and secured the future of the films with the company's backing for a good few years.

Titles Are Everything

The first two films financed by Rank, *Don't Lose Your Head* and *Follow That Camel*, were released without the *Carry On* tag. At the time, John Davis, head of the organization, was afraid of being accused of stealing another company's idea (Anglo Amalgamated financed and distributed the first 13 films). Davis was persuaded otherwise and the tag was re-introduced on future productions, as well as later being added to *Head* and *Camel*.

Producer Peter Rogers came up with the title for each film at home

---

THE RANK ORGANISATION   **STALLS**

Presents

A PETER ROGERS PRODUCTION

PHIL SILVERS   KENNETH WILLIAMS
JIM DALE   CHARLES HAWTREY
JOAN SIMS   ANGELA DOUGLAS

PETER BUTTERWORTH   **BERNARD BRESSLAW**   **ANITA HARRIS**

in

FOLLOW THAT CAMEL
In colour

'A'

Screenplay by Talbot Rothwell

Produced by Peter Rogers

Directed by Gerald Thomas

Press Show: LEICESTER SQUARE THEATRE
Monday, December 11th at 10.30 a.m.
GUEST   Admit One   No Children   *Approximate Running Time 95 mins.*

Carry On ... Follow That Camel. Press and crew screening invitation.

in the bath. The title, of course, immediately suggested the storyline and a plot was formulated, and script subsequently written. Simple.

Wonderful scriptwriters such as Norman Hudis, Talbot Rothwell and Dave Freeman took Rogers' title, with his continuing guidance, and delivered wonderfully funny situations and characters—although Rogers maintains that no part was ever written with an actor in mind. The star of the film was the title, and the cast followed.

The Big Location

The pinnacle of *Carry On* was *Up the Khyber* (1968). Arguably the best in the series, the title appears on the list of the best 100 British films of the century, and rightfully so.

Set in the days of British rule in Imperial India, the story presents Sid James as the affable British Governor Sir Sidney Ruffdiamond, and Kenneth Williams as the Khasi of Khalibad.

Wonderful cast, wonderful story and bloody hard work. We went up to Wales for the Khyber Pass scenes (shot around Snowdonia), and I was up there on my own—in terms of the effects department. Gun shots, a few explosions and the like followed, which was pretty straightforward stuff, with a few black powder charges. Then, when we came home, it became a different kettle of fish completely.

A wall and gate was constructed around the front of the Pinewood mansion, doubling for the British Residence, and Gerry came up to me to say how I had to blow it all up during the final battle.

I said I could do it, providing the plasterers and construction department made the wall up of a fairly light texture as it was only about 30 feet away from the main house, and I didn't want to

Carry On Up the Khyber. **The hilarious dinner sequence where the room just falls apart. (Gareth Owen Collection.)**

blow all the windows out and have the resident producers chasing
me.

I planted soft charges around the wall — which was kilned plaster, in
fact — and set them off in sequence. I was a bit worried, but Gerry
thought it was hilarious fun. It worked rather well. I then had to move
to the interior shots, which turned out to be the most worrying for me.

A Steady Shot

My dear chum Sid James had recently recovered from a heart attack and
had a scene to do which was rather tricky insofar as he had a bottle of
red wine in his hand, and when he went to pour it a bullet smashed it. I
said to Sid that I'd put a little charge in the bottom of the prop bottle,
and a detonator in the cork so as he could smash it himself.

"No son," he said "you can shoot it."

My reaction was something like "golly gosh" as I couldn't believe
what I was hearing. But Sid was adamant.

"With a gun?" I asked.

"Yes, a gun," he said.

Well, there was no way I would have used a real gun and so we com-
promised on a .22 air rifle. All was set such that as Sid tilted the bottle,
the base was sticking out and that was my target. Thank Christ I was a
pretty good shot, that's all I can say.

Gerald gave me the word — I was only about five yards away — and I
fired, smashing the bottle. All of the wine, or colored water, went all
over Sid's shirt.

"Great son, great," said Sid. "We won't need take two, will we,
Gerry?"

"No, I don't think so," came the relieving reply.

The rest of the dinner scene was absolutely hilarious, and filmed with
a rather stiff upper lip on Pinewood's smallest stage. While the British Residence is being stormed, the Governor is resolute that dinner should con-
tinue, and the uprising native Burpas would not spoil it. Cue scenes of
falling plaster, shaking foundations and shattering windows (all orchestrated by Bert), much to the utter amazement of dinner guest Peter Butterworth.

Peter Butterworth and Sid made that scene for me as they were so good.
I didn't action all of the plaster falling and the like, the prop men had to
do that because of the union rules, but I gave them the word. I was in
charge of all the other little gimmicks too (like a record playing Gatling

gun), and the firearms throughout the film … quite exhausting work, but huge fun.

One of the hilarious knock-ons from the film was a letter which Peter Rogers received from a chap who had just been to the cinema. He said that he had served in the actual Khyber Pass when he was in the forces, and how marvelous it was to see it on the big screen, and went on to say how he recognized many of the locations from his time out there. Peter didn't have the heart to write back and say that we never left North Wales, let alone getting as far as Afghanistan!

Spray the Grass Green

Later in the year, the gang headed for the great outdoors and a camping holiday. Thus came *Carry On Camping*. As with all of the other films, this didn't stray far from Pinewood either. About as far as the back (strawberry) field in fact. Despite the many other wonderful sets constructed on site, it is inevitably the glimpse of the now barren field that causes the most gasps of wonder when tours of the studio have been conducted in recent years. The echoes of laughter live on there.

By this time, autumn was approaching and the leaves were falling from the trees. As the film was very much set in the warm summer months, the order went out to paint some green leaves on the trees, and spray the muddy field green too. Green they became! The scene was now set, and up went the tents.

Bert recalls *Camping* as quite probably the film on which he had greatest fun and, with a sigh, the film for which he will be forever remembered as "the phantom bra snatcher."

The fun on the film came very much in the work: Bert cites the team's total professionalism as being a joy for technicians like him. There were no temper tantrums (or certainly none that Peter Rogers allowed to get as far as the floor), no in-fighting and no hanging around.

The schedules were usually six weeks and if they didn't do it in six, then it would be five. Never any longer. All of Peter's productions were tight in terms of time, because they were modest budgets, and we just didn't have endless funds to play around with. They were very efficient, though, never skimping on quality.

Unlike most of Bert's other films up until this time, he was on constant call during the production, not just the odd day or two as had been the case. He was on stage virtually every day.

I had to be. Gerald used to say, "I'd like such and such a thing to happen. Can you get me this?" … "Can you move that?" … it was all that sort of thing and you usually had about ten minutes to do it. So we had to be ready.

The *Carry On*s weren't as serious as the Bonds in that respect, Gerald often added little touches during the shooting as and when he felt they suited. The Bonds were much more planned and locked-down.

That Damn Bra

Perhaps the most famous (or is it infamous?) scene of all the films was in *Camping* and involved Barbara Windsor and a certain supportive garment. Bert takes up the story:

> I can't escape it! I've blown up houses, set streets on fire and kitted out 007 with gadgets; but what do they always ask?
>
> "Aren't you the man who whipped Barbara's bra off?"
>
> Yes, I am!
>
> It was quite a thing at the time in the press, and I read many reports which said that Barbara's bra was pulled off with a fishing rod. Well, I'm sorry but I'm here to tell you it wasn't. It couldn't have been, for that matter.
>
> The scene involved Barbara exercising out on the field with a group of other girls, all being led by Kenneth Williams. In swinging her arms in and out, her chest comes out and wham … off flies her bra.

> A fishing rod could never have done that. Looking at it logically, even though the bra was only loosely stitched at the back, you still needed something like 25 or 30 pounds strain on a thread — a fishing rod couldn't handle that. So I constructed a rig consisting of a spring, release mechanism and a length of piano wire.
>
> Despite what you might think, I never got to see a bleeding thing; I wired up the bra and stood a few feet out of frame with my back to

Carry On Camping. The famous "bra scene" with Barbara Windsor. (Gareth Owen Collection.)

the action. When Gerry said "Now," I pulled the catch and off flew the bra. By the time I turned around, Barbara was all covered over. Damn.

The spring had about 25 pounds of tension behind it and, to be honest, it was the first time I'd used this sort of rig for this purpose, so didn't know how — if at all — it would work. Thankfully, it worked perfectly on the first take, which was just as well as I don't think I'd have gone for another take had it failed. I'd have had to have tried something else. I do remember Barbara being very nervous, though. I won't repeat her exact words, but they were rather choice. She was terrified of showing her boobs.

Pals for Life

The largely Cockney origins of the cast and crew, including Bert, added a little something else special to the productions. The slang, odd swear words and humor were all very much at home with everyone, and a tremendously easy and friendly environment resulted. Quite a contrast to the international make-up of the Bond cast and crew.

Bert made many friends among the cast and became tremendously fond of many of them and he looked forward each year to his five or six weeks of fun with them all.

I was one of them, you see. Sidney [James], Hattie [Jacques] who I still love and miss very much, dear Charlie Hawtrey and Kenny Williams.

I always remember on *Carry On at Your Convenience* we had over 150 toilets outside of our workshops, and Kenny came by one day, nose cocked in the air. He looked at them all and said, in his own inimitable fashion, "Yeesss, I see," and then walked off! He was perhaps one of the more uncertain elements of the cast, as I didn't always know what to expect from him — some days he was tremendously friendly, and on others he was quite removed from us all. But I remember him for the genius he was, and for the pleasure he brought us all.

Hattie was, on the other hand, always so friendly and radiated a warmth that I've never experienced before or since from an actress. She was so very sweet, as was her husband John Le Mesurier. I remember one day Hattie came up to me and asked if I might help, I said if it was humanly possible, then I would. Her son, it transpired, was involved in a carnival at college and had a great big dragon costume. Hattie wondered if I could do anything to get some smoke coming out of its nose.

No problem, said I, and I loaned her one of the workshop's little smoke machines. If I hadn't had one, I'd have made her one — such was the lady. Sadly she died very young, and I'll never really get over it, to be honest. Her death had quite an effect on me, as it did on all those who knew and worked with her.

Bernie Bresslaw was a very nice chap too. Despite his always playing the funny and sometimes bit dopey characters, he was in fact a great intellectual and loved reading when he was waiting for his call. One day I remember he came over to me and said, "'Bert, can you fix my bins for me?"

Being a Cockney, I knew bins were in fact glasses, and he handed them over to me — the glass had dropped out one side of the frame. Within seconds I fixed them and off he went, terribly grateful. I know it doesn't sound like much, but my helping him like that cemented a bond between us. We'd have done anything for one another — not just me and Bernie, but the whole of the cast and crew.

Even though I might not have seen them all much, we were all pals. In a way, a bit like family — you don't see them from one Christmas 'til the next, but you know they're always there for you. That's a marvelous feeling to have, and one you'd be hard pushed to find with many companies nowadays.

Call a Stuntman, Please

The following year, the team returned to the venue of an earlier success (the medical profession): *Carry On Again Doctor*, with Sid James, Hattie Jacques, Kenneth Williams, Joan Sims, Charles Hawtrey and Jim Dale in the lead roles.

Ah, yes, Jim Dale. He was another Norman Wisdom in the respect of him wanting to do all of his own stunts and be involved in all of the effects.

There's a wonderful sequence when Jim and Barbara Windsor are in the X-ray room and Jim attempts to take a picture of Barbara. It all goes badly wrong and the sparks start flying. Jim then decides to pull out the main fuse, and off he runs ...

At the fuse box, he slipped and pulled it all off the wall and it lit up like a Christmas tree. I was terrified because Jim insisted on doing it all himself — with all of those pyrotechnics. I eventually relented, under protest I might add, but pleaded with him to stand well to one side of the fuse box. It's bad enough letting off my fireworks near anyone, but right in front of him would have been unthinkable. He was up for it all the same.

That scene was very effective, and came together very well. From there, though, Jim had to make his way through the various ward corridors; ending up going down stairs on a trolley and through a window. He gave me nightmares at times.

Cutaway shots were planned for the fuse box sequence, whereby the director could show the knock-on effects on Dale's on-screen incompetence with the electrics. One such cutaway featured on "old dear" (Lucy Griffiths) sitting upright in bed, knitting whilst listening to the hospital radio on a set of headphones.

Gerry asked me if I could arrange for the headphones to seemingly blow up on her head, and a puff of smoke emerge. Sounds easy, but when you're playing with something on an actress' head, there are certain safety factors to take into account.

I asked if the lady had been made aware of the potential dangers. She could have had her hearing damaged, or even have her hair catch fire.

"Well, can you make sure that doesn't happen?" they said.

Great isn't it? They have all the wild ideas and I have to sort it all out safely, without impairing on the look of it all.

I made the headphones myself, and had a long chat with Lucy, who was a wonderful little lady, and explained that all I was going to do was blow a puff of smoke out; there wouldn't be any bang or noise. I inserted a little bit of powder in the 'phones and set it off to cue. Very nerve-wracking.

That's one thing people don't realize actually: We effects men are responsible in the eyes of the insurance companies for carrying out procedures safely and competently. So we have to be extra, extra careful or they'd close us down — they have the power to do that. Needless to say, when we have a tricky sequence to arrange, we're fully aware that it's not just about the safety of people involved in that sequence, but the continuation of the whole film too.

On Safari

Later in the year, the gang re-grouped and prepared themselves for a jungle adventure, but alas, locations weren't as exotic as the title suggests, as *Carry On Up the Jungle* was, again, filmed entirely on Pinewood's stages.

I guess there were more effects and gimmicks on that than any other *Carry On* film.

Frankie Howard was on his second *Carry On* (after *Doctor*), and it was the first time I'd met him, actually. He was very quiet and subdued most of the time, and seemed to fit in well with the rest of the team.

THE RANK ORGANISATION   **STALLS**

presents

A PETER ROGERS PRODUCTION

FRANKIE HOWERD   SIDNEY JAMES

CHARLES HAWTREY   JOAN SIMS   TERRY SCOTT

KENNETH CONNOR   BERNARD BRESSLAW

JACKI PIPER

in

CARRY ON UP THE JUNGLE

In Colour

Screenplay by	*Produced by* PETER ROGERS	*Directed by*
TALBOT ROTHWELL		*GERALD THOMAS*

Trade Show: Studio One, Oxford Street
Wednesday, 8th April, at 10.30 a.m.

GUEST   Admit One   No Children   Approximate Running Time 95 mins.

Carry On Up the Jungle invitation.

Early on in the film, Sid James is in the camp that had been set up for the night deep in the jungle, carrying his double barrel shotgun over his arm, un-cocked. Meanwhile, Joan Sims is in the make-shift shower. Of course, Sid being Sid, or rather his usual "Sid" character in the films, took a peek at Joan in the shower. It was then that the script called for the rifle barrel to raise itself to a total erect position, if you know what I mean, and was very much completely cocked, as we say in gun circles.

Gerry said that he wanted the rifle to do this little trick, and could I do it for him? Never one to say no, I said I'd have a go.

It wasn't as easy as it sounded and I asked for a little time on this one, and Gerry kindly said I could take as long as I liked — but we had a fortnight. Story of my life!

Well, I thought about it and about the different ways it might have been possible, but it wasn't practical half the time. Then, one night lying in bed, it hit me. *I'd* have to make the rifle, and make it very light-weight and not the usual 12-bore weight.

I made a replica out of aluminum, sprayed it and attached a wire cable, the sort one has on motorcycles for the clutch and brake controls. It ran from the tip of the barrel up Sid's sleeve, round his shoulder and down his back, then it ran down his trouser leg, out across the ground and over to my little lever contraption. When Gerry said the word, I pulled my lever, applied a tension to the cable and up popped the barrel. It worked every time, and is tremendously funny to watch in the film.

You don't see the cable and my lever on screen, of course, but that would have probably added to the comedy — the things we used to do!

Bert's assignments on the film were far from over at this stage, for next came a request to design and make a large insect.

Gerry told me about this great big butterfly that he wanted to fly about and then settle on a particular rock on the set. There was no way we'd have ever got a real one to do it, it was just impossible. How do you train a butterfly?

"Well, can you make one?" asked Gerry "I want it to be quite large, be able to flap its wings and look fairly realistic."

I said I could do it — I'm far too eager to please, that's my trouble!— and set about drawing this fictitious butterfly with an eight-inch wing span, and body of about four inches long and an inch wide. It had to be fictitious as we didn't want people to recognize a rare or protected species, or accuse us of being cruel in any way.

I inserted a rubber bulb inside a butterfly body I'd made in my workshop based on pictures and sketches in nature books; coming out of which I had a very fine tube leading to a bigger bulb which, in turn, was controlled for inflating and deflating with a few little levers. As I moved the levers, the air went in and out of the large bulb — and the hence the smaller one contained inside the body — causing the hinged wings to move. In order to achieve that action, I ran very fine wires (almost like little veins) through the wings and the other ends were attached to the length of the body. As the bulb (body) inflated, the wire tension was decreased and the wings opened. Conversely, as it deflated the wires were stretched and caused the wings to close.

We flew the butterfly around the set using fishing rods, and then set it down on the rock. I was a few feet away with my levers and off we went...

That wasn't Bert's last scene with "creatures" in the film, as he was next asked to create an Oozlum bird.

Ah, dear Ozzie, he was great fun. The art director asked me if I could make this Oozlum bird. I had been in the Air Force and knew what it was, but had no idea what it looked like. The old story was that the Oozlum flew around in ever decreasing circles and eventually disappeared up its own … well, it's own rear orifice.

Bert was told that the design was open to a certain amount of interpretation, but should have a rear end of about four inches round, with lots of fur around. It also had to nod, turn and tilt its head.

It wasn't really that difficult. Ozzie was about two feet high, actually, and the engineering part was fairly straightforward, with a couple of motors and remotely connected controls. I made a little model of the bird and the plastering department then made the main body for me. Then came the job of finding the feathers. But where the heck do you get lots of colorful feathers?

I wanted to use real feathers—which probably complicated matters for myself—and I ended up going to a company in the City of London which made ladies hats.

I'd already acquired a shocking name for strange requests in the locale of Pinewood, and was now set to take it further afield.

I met the milliner, who was tucked away in a smallish room in a three story house, and told him that I wanted some white, blue, red, yellow, pink and so on, feathers.

"How many?" he asked.

"About four of five hundred should do it."

"How many hats are you making?" he inquired.

I told him that I wasn't making hats, but a bird. He asked what sort of bird, so I told him — an Oozlum. Of course, he then wanted to know what an Oozlum was. So I told him.

Needless to say, I got some very funny looks. I don't think he could believe his ears. He must have thought I'd escaped from somewhere. Had it not been for the fact I had cash in my hand to pay for them, I probably would have been "removed" from the premises.

I eventually got all the feathers I needed, and Ozzie was created. He went down a treat, and looked wonderful. In fact, he surpassed my expectations too. After filming, I kept him in my workshop, and he often became a conversation point with visitors. Foolishly, when I retired, I didn't take him with me. We all live and learn, don't we?

Another "animal" encounter came during the famous dinner scene in the film, where a snake sneaks up Joan Sims' dress. She in turn thought it was one of the assembled gentleman diners showing a little more than passing affection — which she didn't seem averse to, it must be said.

It was in fact a rubber snake. And I had to pull that bloody thing with a piece of string, right up Joan's leg and … well, further up, if you get my meaning. It sounds funny now, I know, but it's not a very pleasant thing to request of an artiste — do you mind if I shove my head up your skirt?

More standard gimmicks and effects were then called for when the script mentioned a little explosion, of sorts.

There's a scene where our gang are captured by cannibals in the jungle, and someone throws a burning torch into a box of ammunition that's lying there, prompting all hell to break loose.

Gerry said, "We need a good explosion with a few charges replicating the cartridges going off — but nothing too big."

The Oozlum bird from *Carry On Up the Jungle.*

He turned to Bert with a questioning look.

Right, I said, leave it to me. In truth, I think I was a little too over-enthusiastic — much like my firework parties — as I made the explosions a little too big. Well, much too big.

All the charges went off to cue and created quite a deafening noise. After it had all calmed down, Gerry came over to me.

"Were they little charges?"

"Yes," I said.

"I'd hate to be around when you used big ones then," he exclaimed. But wasn't it good on film?!

One of the notable trivia about the gang's sojourn into jungle territory was the vast expanse of jungle foliage created in Pinewood's workshops. Most was plastic-based and tended to melt under the tremendous heat of the lights on the stage!

Holiday Time

One of the next *Carry On*s on which Bert had a significant involvement, *Carry On Abroad* required another "little" explosion.

The whole story is about this hotel that's still being built in the tourist area of Elsbels and, quite honestly, ready to fall apart. The team have the misfortune to go over for a little holiday.

Towards the end of the film, the hotel really does crumble, but the characters are all so drunk that they think it's all part of the party. Poor Peter Butterworth is the hotel owner, frantically trying to persuade everyone to evacuate, but they're not having any of it.

Gerry said he wanted one of the pillars in the room to crumble and fall, giving way to all manner of muck from the ceiling. That was a bit tricky.

What I did was to plant a small charge at the base of the pillar, which was actually just kilned plaster, and said that when I detonated it, it would probably jump up a few inches and then topple over and smash into little pieces. So actors beware.

"Great," said Gerry "But don't make it too big an explosion, will you?"

As if I would, eh?

Anyway, it was all rigged and I told Gerry to make sure the actors were well away from the area when he gave me the word. Up came my cue and I pressed the button.

The pillar jumped about six inches in the air and came back down and landed in exactly the same spot — I'd never seen anything like it before in my life. There it was, standing perfectly perpendicular.

I couldn't have done that if I'd tried. It just stood there. The cameras were still rolling, as there was collective chaos all around the set for this scene, and to stop it to do a re-take on the pillar would have meant re-staging the whole lot. But dear Peter Butterworth had seen what had happened and he edged over to the pillar and leaned against it, in character, and it toppled over and smashed. It actually worked brilliantly with him doing it like that, as it was very convincing. I'm so pleased we had such quick-thinking and professional actors on the set. He certainly saved my bacon.

The *Carry On*s were 100 percent fun: fun to make and fun to watch. They weren't intended to carry any political messages, slants nor hidden meanings. What you see is what you get. That, Bert maintains, was the secret of their success.

The chemistry worked, the scripts worked and the casting worked. What more could you ask for?

I had terrific fun on the *Carry On*s and made some wonderful friends. I'll forever remember dear old Sid James, who to many epitomized everything of the best in the *Carry On*s, and how he used to come over in the morning with the racing page of the newspapers. He'd always ask me "what I fancied." I wasn't really a gambling man, and he knew that, so I didn't know much about horse racing; but he'd then start rattling off a few names and I'd tell him the ones I liked the sound of.

"Do you?" he'd ask. "Right."

I never knew if he won or not.

Camping Again

One of the last bangs Bert had to organize in the series came with *Carry On Behind* (1976). Again set on a campsite, but this time backing onto an archaeological dig, Bert was quite literally charged with blowing up a tent.

The idea was that a little gas stove was thrown into this girl's tent by Jack Douglas, and in him doing so, he accidentally knocked the valve on, and gas was heard to be leaking out. A short time afterwards Windsor Davies [Jack's mate in the caravan] tossed his cigarette out of the window, and it landed very near the tent. Bang!

Gerry said that he didn't want anything too big, just the tent blown into the air.

"Yes, Gerry, I know exactly what you mean," said I, with a twinkle in my eye.

I didn't see Gerry's reaction to my enthusiasm, but knowing that he knew me pretty well by now, guessed it probably involved a raised eyebrow or two.

First things first, though. I had to do something about the camping stove. We weren't allowed to use one that looked like a famous brand one, as we were suggesting it was faulty in the scene, and that could lead to all sorts of legal complications. So, the first thing I did was to find a gas canister that was empty and that didn't have a unique shape, suggesting a certain brand. I then sprayed it bright orange. There weren't any orange gas stoves out on the market then, and that covered our backs.

Next, I attached three four-inch "bursters" into the tent — one either end and the other hanging in the middle from the support pole.

Gerry gave the word, and I detonated them all at once. I think I'd gone a bit over the top again, to be honest, as the tent was blown to smithereens. Typical of an effects man, ask for an explosion and you certainly get one! But as the debris landed on the ground, I noticed that the center burster hadn't detonated. The cameras were still rolling too, so it was obviously caught in frame.

Gerry was quite happy with the shot and said "marvelous, great, thanks" and walked away.

I followed him and quietly pointed out the unexploded burster, which I thought might have spoiled the scene. Gerry was completely un-bothered, and said

"Don't worry, it's a nightlight in the tent!"

He really was very clever like that, and was able to walk around certain things that perhaps didn't make sense in the strictest definition of the word. He was very clever in his editing, kept things moving and turned problems into spurs for inventiveness.

Another sequence came about after it was discovered that the caravan site was in fact on a field that was subsiding quite considerably — into the ruins of Roman remains in fact (hence the archaeological dig substory). The script called for Jack Douglas to unwittingly step out of his caravan into a great — and deep — pool of water. The hole was dug, but before "action!" was called, Gerald Thomas insisted on having the water warmed.

That's the sort of bloke he was; bloody thoughtful. I never once heard him raise his voice or lose his patience with anyone. He was quite unique in that respect.

The Final Few

Although Bert had been involved in the next of the series, *Carry On England* in 1976, his input was more or less in straightforward gimmicks (including a small bang and puff of smoke or two) and the odd run-of-the-mill effect — nothing really on the scale of the above-mentioned, which stand out as being the most important and enjoyable, as far as Bert is concerned.

In 1978, Rogers compiled *That's Carry On* which, he admitted, came from the idea of the MGM compilation *That's Entertainment*. Its success led the team to thinking about other possibilities.

Meanwhile, and mindful of the more explicit *Confessions* films with Robin Asquith, *Carry On Emmanuelle* was put into production with backing from Hemdale. The idea was to make an X-rated *Carry On* sending up the soft porn Sylvia Kristel films. Suzanne Danielle was cast in the lead role alongside Kenneth Williams, Kenneth Connor, Peter Butterworth, Joan Sims and Jack Douglas. Barbara Windsor had earlier refused to take part in the film due to what she described as being "an awful script." The film fared poorly with critics and audiences alike.

Meanwhile, the compilation film's success led to Rogers setting up two TV series of classic *Carry On* clips: *That's Carry On* and *What a Carry On*. They were both extremely successful. Although the 1980s was a *Carry On* feature-free decade, the compilations kept the team busy as each series took an estimated nine months to complete. After all, there were hundreds of thousands of feet of film to sift through.

One or two feature ideas were mooted, with *Carry On Down Under* nearly getting underway before one of the financiers involved flitted with all of the money. However, in 1992 it was announced that *Carry On Columbus* was set to go into production with producer John Goldstone, director Gerald Thomas and executive producer Peter Rogers. Bert regrets having retired before *Carry On Columbus* moved into production, because in fact it turned out to be Gerald Thomas' last film before his 1993 death. However, Bert admits that in many ways, he was perhaps best missing out on the film, as so many of the old faces and friends had sadly since departed. Making a *Carry On* without them wouldn't have been the same. The new faces of Rik Mayall, Julian Clary, Alexei Sayle and Sara Crowe was augmented by old regulars Jim Dale, Bernard Cribbins, Leslie Phillips, June Whitfield and Jack Douglas, but the chemistry just wasn't there anymore.

It's doubtful that there will ever be another *Carry On* film, but Peter Rogers—now well into his eighties—hopes to perhaps make a TV film with the *Carry On* prefix. But the 31 films that were all made at Pinewood hold a place in film history and in countless people's hearts—especially Bert's.

SCENE SIX

The Air Disaster and Magical Illusions!

On March 29, 1969, the newspaper headlines read:

Mayday … Mayday … Plane Crash on Slough

Twenty-three people were reported killed and 40 others injured when an Aero Costa Brava Viscount airliner bound for Heathrow from Madrid crashed on an office block and four houses at 10:05 A.M.

It was something Slough had been fearing for years, as it was the major town nearest to Heathrow airport, directly under the incoming flight path.

What did this have to do with Bert Luxford? Quite a lot, in fact, as he was responsible … or, more precisely, he was responsible for creating the illusion of an air disaster in Slough, for that is what it was. But it was not for a film. A week or two before the crash was to take place, Bert was called in to see Pinewood's Managing Director, Kip Herren, for a "hush-hush" briefing.

Kip had been approached by Chief Superintendent Ted Evans of the Metropolitan Police, who was himself head of C-Division which had responsibility for Slough, Windsor and Maidenhead, regarding an exercise they wanted to carry out in Slough.

Planning a Disaster

Several months of talks had taken place between the chiefs of fire, ambulance and hospital services and the result was operation "Goldflight" (so named as there were to be several mock gold bars on the plane). The idea was test the resources and response times of the medical, fire and police services should such an accident really occur. It was for all intents and purposes a simulation of an actual air disaster, in every definition of the word.

Ted Evans said he wanted me to organize this disaster they had been planning in Slough. My immediate response was rather choice to say the least! Then, he explained further. They intended to use the large Wellington Shopping Arcade which was then under construction and was really just a concrete shell. There, they wanted to detonate a large explosion that would be heard for miles and also produce thick, black, towering smoke.

The call was then to go out that an airplane had crashed in Slough.

The whole exercise was very well-planned as 60 members of the "Casualty Union" were drafted in to play dead and injured passengers, lying in the roadway and around surrounding buildings amid the wreckage, scattered belongings and cargo. Fake blood was smeared on the roadways near the "dead." And high up on the roof of the building, a corpse slumped over the parapet, along with a number of injured people stranded up there. It was un-nervingly real, but then again, that was the intention.

I was told that my work would be quite simple in essence. Whenever anyone said "simple" to me, I always gave a little chuckle; I knew full well that their ideas of what was and wasn't simple were usually very different to mine, and actual reality.

The wreckage, cargo and belongings were all taken care of by the authorities and, just like on a film, were brought on to dress the "set" very early on the morning of the action, thereby minimizing local interest and nosey-parker interference. That all done, the rest was left to Bert.

They wanted me to create the big "bang" at 10 A.M. precisely. I said I could do it, no problem, providing there wasn't anyone around who might get in the way.

"Oh don't worry, my men will keep the streets clear," I was told.

I'm not naturally cynical, but I do always plan for the worst case scenario, and here that would have been if a member of the public wandered into the immediate area of the explosion. I was only going to use

A scene from the Slough Air Disaster orchestrated by Bert.

"bursters" which aren't anything like real explosives, but can still give a very nasty burn. It might well have turned into a real disaster!

Bursters and Smoke

Bert organized ten eight-inch bursters and a number of smoke pots. His young protégé from the St. John's Ambulance cadet force, Linda, lent him a hand in the safety aspects; for instance, holding onto the fuses while Bert planted the bursters, so as no "well-meaning" passer by could accidentally set one off.

That's a golden rule. Never let any fuses or triggers out of your sight because you always get some fool who'll think he's helping and picks them up, or presses a trigger … well, it doesn't bear thinking about. So Linda was very valuable in that respect.

I planted the bombs in peat, to absorb the explosion better, fairly close together in a circle. I wired it all up for 9 A.M., and was raring to go. The smoke pots were wired up too. Meanwhile, no one in Slough knew what was about to happen.

Then it started to rain, and heavily too. It made me a little anxious, to be honest. That anxiety wasn't misplaced, in fact, as when 10 A.M. came around, I pressed the button and, well, nothing happened!

My first reaction was to think that the circuitry had been affected by the water, but then it hit me ... I had made a little mistake, and it wasn't the water. As I had connected the bursters and smoke canisters to the same detonation circuit, and battery, I never thought about the current they would draw. I realized that I had too much connected to the one battery, and the current reaching each of the devices in the circuit wasn't strong enough to detonate them.

Foolishly, I went over to the bursters and smoke canisters to rewire them. I could have caused myself a nasty injury had anything gone wrong as the battery was still connected to the circuit! I quickly rewired them and, at two minutes past ten, I hit the button again. BANG!

A few moments later the thick black pall of smoke started rising. It was all very realistic, let me tell you.

Alarm

Within minutes, the alarm was raised, and sirens could be heard converging on Slough from all directions. Fire engines were the first to arrive, followed by an ambulance crew. The sheer magnitude of the disaster was far beyond the capabilities of a single crew, but they assisted the injured as best as they could awaiting further back-up.

Fire hoses sprayed foam into the building to extinguish the (supposed) fuel tank fires, and the high turntable engines soon arrived to help officers reach the injured on top of the buildings. Passersby were appalled and disturbed by the scene, several vomiting in the gutters.

For the next hour, emergency services from neighboring towns rushed to Slough and the injured were taken to nearby Wexham Park Hospital.

Meanwhile, the first fire officer to enter the inner sanctum of Bert's explosion area was not amused at what he witnessed.

"What bloody arsehole did all this?" he shouted.

I slowly disappeared further and further back into the crowd and feigned total ignorance! I hate to think what he'd have done to me had I been identified to him — well, at least before he was told it was an exercise and not for real.

The exercise was over. Ted Evans' thoughts: "It was fairly satisfactory. Inevitably there were some mistakes, but then, it was something which, thank goodness, we've not had to deal with before. A lot of lessons have been learned and if the real thing happened, we'd be better prepared for it."

He was not, however, greeted with much enthusiasm from several Slough residents who maintained that he had no right to instigate such an exercise without warning, as it could have caused serious knock-on effects, such as people suffering heart attacks, for instance. But, Evans argued, little (if any) warning would be given if it happened for real.

Fortunately, it hasn't.

A favorable report went back to Pinewood on Bert's involvement, but he was criticized for being 20 seconds late on pressing the trigger.

> It was more like two minutes actually, so I never argued with him. But I think I achieved the desired effect and I have to say I was very impressed with the way the "casualties" acted. I know they were all professionals, but they certainly convinced me of their injuries which, of course, were the result of some fantastic makeup.

The Art of Illusion

Bert has always had a fascination for magic and illusions, going right back into his youth, and he did, perhaps inevitably, become rather accomplished at some illusions and tricks himself. Therefore, when top-rated TV entertainers David Nixon and Ali Bongo walked into his workshop to talk about him building some props for their magic show, Bert was thrilled.

> First and foremost, I must warn you that I am not going to give away any secrets of how tricks are done. I don't believe in that at all. I hate it when people come onto television explaining how tricks are done and illusions created. Why to they feel they have to do that?
>
> I was fascinated with the likes of Dante and Houdini when I grew up. I think that in explaining how they did their tricks would not only have spoiled the entertainment for me and others like me — and these people are entertainers, after all — but would have also been unethical. Magicians and illusionists spend years perfecting their work, and that work should be respected. The audience wants to be thrilled, mystified and entertained. If you take away the first two by divulging the secrets, there is little left of the third.
>
> All I will say on the matter is that the art of illusion is not necessarily in what you see, but in what you don't see. So remember that.
>
> I digress. When David and Ali came in to talk to me, they wanted a construction, or box if you like, which would enable them to make a lady disappear.

David Nixon was very famous and popular on TV at this time through his show, which was watched by millions; whereas Ali Bongo, aside from his TV appearances, was most famous for being the chief mover and shaker at the Magic Circle in London, which, I might add, has expelled several people for giving away magic secrets!

Ali had this design for the box, which wasn't over-complicated in its working, but rather ingenious in its conception. As usual, I just had a sketch to go on.

The idea was that the young lady in question would climb into the box, which had to be made out of glass, and would be covered over with a black sheet. David would then fire a blank firing pistol, the sheet would raise up and, hey presto, the young lady had vanished!

It took me a few weeks to complete the box, which was nothing great to look at. But, although modesty prevails, it worked bloody marvelously.

Not too long after, another member of the magic circle, Paul Daniels, descended on the studio—again with Ali Bongo. Interestingly, Daniels had bought Roger Moore's house in Denham (a few minutes drive from Pinewood) after the James Bond star had left Britain to become a tax exile. Bert had often helped Moore with various bits and pieces of entertainment at his house over the years, and so it was familiar territory.

We had a chat about all that, and then another fascinating construction was described to me. Another box. This time, however, a much smaller table-top one about two feet by two feet by two feet. Paul intended to use it in a routine during which he was going to produce all sorts things out of it: rabbits, birds, long colorful cloths and so on. The funny thing is, when we made the box and placed it on a table to try it out, the first thing people did was look under the table it was on. Some people are very suspicious, aren't they? But not one of them could figure it out.

But is the art of illusion only in the sleight of wrist? No, not quite.

I'm sure you know that the majority, if not all, of the most successful illusionists are blessed with the gift of the gab. They come onto the stage and hold the audience, captivated, almost straight away. They hold this attention throughout and that's important, very important, because you have to guide your audience into seeing what you want them to see and nothing more. Paul is marvelous at doing that. That's a very big part of his success and of his magic. There's a lot going on during all of his patter, but not so as you'd notice.

We completed the box, and off they went with it — very pleased again, I might add. Fortunately, I caught the show on TV where Paul used the prop, and I will call it a prop in this instance ... all sorts came out of it, ending up with the obligatory pretty girl.

Knowing how it was done spoiled the illusion a little for me, I guess, but those watching it on TV with me were totally mystified by it all, and totally entertained. That's why I'm so determined as to not tell anyone how its done. More often than not it results in disappointment, so why do it?

It was a fascinating period, and I really enjoyed working on the illusions for David and Paul because, quite honestly, it wasn't work for me — it was play time again. The interesting thing I've learned from my association with the Magic Circle is that most modern illusions are reworkings, or revamps, if you like, of older illusions. What you see nowadays may have been 50 years in the making ... bit by bit they're added to, improved upon and even made more spectacular. That is the, as they say, magic.

Scene Seven

Fire, Rain, the Loch Ness Monster and a Sex Shop!

Things started to heat up for Bert when he was asked to work on *The Firechasers*, with Keith Barron starring as an insurance investigator on the trail of an arsonist.

I had to set Brentford docks alight for the climax! It's now a marina, but back then it was all desolate warehouses and the like. It wasn't just a case of a bit of smoke, but a controlled fire with something like ten 100-pound bottles of propane, in a building that was completely alight from top to bottom. That was probably the biggest fire job I ever did.

My 14-year-old son came with me during one of the night shoots up there, as I suggested he might like to see what Dad did for a living. In the event, the poor little thing was petrified of it all. He never played with matches after that either!

I had to set alight this three-story building, and it was really the first fire job I'd done on this scale. I had all the propane bottles and gas jets blowing out of the windows and on the top of the building. My young colleague, John Richardson, had the Dante Inferno on the roof too—a fire machine which had jets, each burning 10 gallons of paraffin a minute.

The fire service, who were obviously working closely with the production, sent down four of the biggest engines in the country. Boy, did we need 'em. But we soon discovered that the engines couldn't pump water out of the dock directly, as their hoses weren't long enough. So we were limited to what they had in their on-board tanks.

Areas of buildings some 100 foot square were set on fire, creating an intense heat. Then came the Dante machine's input. The scene was phenomenal.

The actual shoot was over in ten minutes and the fire engines drew in to extinguish the flames.

That was a bugger as the poor firemen were on ladders about 100 foot off the ground, with gallons and gallons of water firing out over the flames. It was very difficult to extinguish them as, you see, they weren't real flames, but simulated ones—which are ten times worse! One of the firemen got hurt slightly, if I remember correctly, but nothing too serious, thank goodness.

Looking at the funny side of things, after the shoot, when all the flames were extinguished, we came out of the building congratulating each other. Little did we realize that all of the water that had been poured into the building had now come down to the ground level and frozen in the subzero night time temperatures. The firemen were slithering and sliding all over.

Inferno

In another sequence a warehouse full of clothes is set ablaze. There were rows and rows of garments throughout the building, on rails and shelves, and so Bert took a can of petroleum jelly up each row, up the walls and all around them — rather generously — and stood back.

I asked the director if he was ready. I got the okay, and ran right down to the bottom of the warehouse with my lit torch. I bopped it on the end of the last row, and ran up and down the others (I could run rather fast in those days!). Within 15 seconds it was a veritable inferno. I don't think I could do it now; I can't run for one thing, but it was pretty dangerous too, and truthfully, I was a little anxious, shall we say, when I was lighting the jelly, as had the wind changed I could have easily been trapped. You don't really think about that too much when you're in the thick of it, though, striving to get the best out of a scene.

It did look good, but I don't think that would have been much consolation to my loved ones had anything happened.

Flying

A brief stint on *Guns at Batasi* with Richard Attenborough followed hot on the heels of *Firechasers*, with the "usual old guns, ricocheting, explosions and that sort of thing" before Bert started work on the star-studded *Those Magnificent Men in their Flying Machines*, the story of a newspaper baron sponsoring a 1910 London-to-Paris air race.

Oh, that was great fun. We had Terry-Thomas, Eric Sykes, Gert Frobe, Robert Morley ... the cast list went on and on. The director was Ken Annakin, who was known throughout the studio as Panicking Annakin. His name certainly suited — bloody marvelous director as he was, but he did tend to panic a bit. He'd already made quite a lot of films at Pinewood, for Rank and Disney, and went on to do some other great pictures including *The Longest Day* and *Battle of the Bulge*.

I guess I was more involved in the engineering side of the odd (and I mean odd in the sense of strange here) flying machine. I suppose there were eight or ten of us that made the ground-based replica machines. I must have been involved in that aspect of the picture for six months or more. There was a heck of a lot of model work, which I wasn't involved in as such, and an amazing amount of flying sequences staged at the studio. It proved quite tricky at times with the rear projection techniques we had at our disposal.

What of that all-star cast?

They were all great fun, but dear old Gert Frobe — whom I worked with on *Goldfinger* and *Chitty Chitty Bang Bang* — was particularly wonderful and was in fact, I learnt, a great comic actor. Not many people realized that, especially given his performance as a villain in the Bond film, but it was true. He relished his comedy scenes in the film and I remember that wonderful one where he had to get into the plane for the first time. He pulled out a book "How to Fly" and started reading from it.

"First, get into the cockpit!"

His delivery was sheer perfection, and hysterical!

The Duke

In 1963, one of Hollywood's most famous actors made his first and only film at Pinewood: John Wayne starred in Samuel Bronston's production of *Circus World* with Rita Hayworth. Many of the circus interiors were brought to life at the studio, and Bert was drafted in as special effects advisor.

I'd obviously seen quite a lot of John Wayne's early films as a youngster, and he was quite a hero of mine, so you can imagine how I felt about working with him. I have to say, he didn't disappoint as he was a charming man. I would go as far as saying he was a very placid man actually, and quite the opposite of some of the more famous larger-than-life characters he played on screen.

I was heavily involved with the wire sequences, whereby John was suspended or protected whilst up in the air, and supervised all of that — the actual attaching of wires and insuring that they were safe to use. John was very much involved in the stunts and did pretty much the majority of them himself.

We struck up quite a little friendship and enjoyed playing cards between takes and set-ups. Nothing elaborate or for money, just for the fun of it.

One of the other memorable people I met on set was Coco the Clown, who was a professional clown brought in to teach some of the actors the basics of clowning around. It's not as easy as it sounds and, with the big hats and shoes that they had to wear, was actually quite tricky.

Coco wandered down to the back of the set where I was standing-by one day, after obviously seeing me around the place for a while, and said, "I fancy a cup of tea, would you care to join me?"

I said I'd love to and we then had a very pleasant conversation. During which I mentioned that I'd watched him quite a lot on set and wondered if it was all as lovely to do as it was to see; he always looked so happy and made the children laugh.

"Making them laugh is the hardest thing you can do," he replied, emotionally.

I'll never forget that.

Liar Liar

Based on Keith Waterhouse's West End hit, *Billy Liar* was a very imaginative and thought-provoking film. Tom Courtenay played the eponymous Billy who lives in a bit of a daydream world, a far cry from his job as a funeral director's clerk.

His imagination ran wild at wild at times and found him as a dictator in Ruritania, or perhaps pitted against prehistoric dinosaurs for example.

Ah, yes, the dinosaurs. They were actually made by me. This was 1963, you must remember and we're not exactly talking *Jurassic Park* by any means, not even Ray Harryhausen's ingenious stop-motion techniques. I

***Billy Liar:* The dinosaurs made by Bert.**

made about five models which were about three foot by two foot in size (I still have one, in fact) and static. They were made out of Fiberglas from molds I modeled. It was quite a long-winded process that took weeks, for perhaps a few seconds of screen time. But that's the movie business for you.

Chitty

In 1967, Albert R. Broccoli elected to make a film based on one of Ian Fleming's non–Bond stories. In fact, it was quite a departure for the author, as he moved out of the world of international espionage, exotic locations and beautiful women to a fantasy children's story which Fleming had penned while recovering from a heart attack.

Chitty Chitty Bang Bang is remembered with tremendous affection at Pinewood, and by Bert also. Again, he worked with production designer Ken Adam in realizing the many gimmicks and effects.

I worked on it for six months or more, primarily on the car, which was made by Ford. There were about four cars in all. Two were roadworthy

Chitty Chitty Bang Bang: **The car today, still a crowd puller. (Robin Harbour.)**

and the others were constructed for certain sequences such as water, flying and so forth. It was, like the DB5, a big team effort. It would have been impossible for one person to achieve what was required, impossible.

I think there were five of us who worked on the main car — John Stears, myself, Ronnie Ballinger, Frank George and an electronics man — which is still in existence.

The water sequences which used the hydrofoil gimmick were filmed in Southampton, and Ronnie Ballinger and I were responsible for that one. The flying car — with the wings and other gimmicks — was used mainly at Pinewood.

There was a lot of complicated model work on the film, too, which I wasn't involved in, apart from the big Zeppelin, that is. I did a little bit on that.

It's quite a funny story actually, as Ken had designed a model for use in the film, but was approached by a couple of balloonists who claimed that not only could they do it for real, but for a comparable price. Ken, obviously, said, "Okay let's try it." What he didn't say was that his design was based on a French airship — and one that never got off the ground!

These two guys were as keen as mustard, though, and built the airship, but were a little nervous about the motor on it. They took it out into Hampshire for some test flights, and met with a little accident out there, pulling down some power lines on the way. Half the farmers in Hampshire threatened to sue United Artists [the film's backer] because they couldn't use their milking equipment!

Bert became quite emotional when recalling his work on the film, and the many wonderful people involved in the cast and crew — not least Dick Van Dyke and director Ken Hughes. Among his other tasks was the design and mechanical operations of the "boxes" that were used to protect the

The *Chitty* Zeppelin.

Queen from Gert Frobe's evil villain. The boxes themselves were big enough to hold an adult and out of them jump our heroes (Dick Van Dyke and Sally Anne Howes). Bert confesses that whenever he runs the film nowadays, he wishes he could still be on that set, over and above any other that he has worked on.

Harry Palmer

A complete contrast to the previous assignments came with Bert's next film, working again with production designer Ken Adam and producer Harry Saltzman.

The Ipcress File was one of Michael Caine's big success stories. He was a Cockney, lower-class James Bond in it. I didn't do much in the way of big effects, more of the, dare I say, menial work such as opening and closing doors on cue. I was constantly on call, and raring to go if

On location for *Funeral in Berlin*: Bert, Frank George and the Berlin bear.

needed. It wasn't very scientific, more routine servicing. However, for the follow-up film *Funeral in Berlin*, I was very much involved. In fact, an incident occurred on that film which will haunt me for the rest of my days.

The Cold War was at its height and the Berlin Wall was very much in evidence. Such was the situation that functioning guns could not be taken out there, not even blank-firing. Full stop. Additionally, you have to remember that they were filming just a few yards away from the wall.

Frank George and I took over some small gas-firing guns which consisted of a model gun connected to a pipe through which a mixture of oxygen and acetylene [flowed]. They didn't make a noise, but "sparked" as though firing, so the actual bang could be dubbed later very effectively.

The guns were very uncomfortable for the actors as the pipes carrying the mixture were fed from the guns up their arms, across their chests, down their legs and to the tanks. The mixture was fired by an electrical sparkplug in the barrel, activated by pressing the trigger.

Several scenes involved the shooting of people attempting to get over the wall by the (then) East German soldiers. Many tried, but few made it across alive.

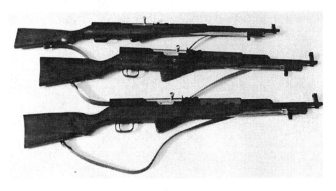

Funeral in Berlin: The gas guns.

The director, Guy Hamilton, was setting up an escape sequence over the wall involving a very large four-foot-tall metal bucket. He said to Frank and me, "I want one of you two to get into this large bucket, which will be lifted by a crane over the wall, and have bullet holes fired through it on the way."

Charming, said I, absolutely charming, as they all looked at me!

We drilled holes in the bucket and covered them over with a bit of plaster (painted the same color as the bucket, obviously) and a tube sat behind each hole. In each tube we inserted a small detonator and gun cotton. Each of the detonators was connected to a firing board which was, in fact, a row of nails in a block of wood connected to a 12-volt battery. To detonate, a firing rod was run along the nails. This simulated the effect of gunfire hitting the bucket. The faster one went across the nails, the quicker the bullets appeared to hit the bucket! It was a simple set-up, but one in which I nearly broke my leg, as during the running and jumping into the bucket I hit my leg with a real force on the side of the thing, and was in agony with it. In the best traditions of show business, I had to carry on for the take.

The Sten Guns

At very short notice, on location, Bert was commissioned to make a gas-firing Sten Gun. While it was tricky getting the smaller gas rifles into East Berlin, it was practically impossible (and illegal) to take a gun of that nature into the Eastern section. Not one to be outwitted, Bert suggested that since it was illegal to bring one in, it might be less complicated if they could get hold of one in East Berlin. It was still risky, but a risk they were prepared to take. Less risky, Bert suggested, might be to make one themselves.

They needed a workshop. Going to just any old place with plans to make a Sten Gun would have undoubtedly caused more problems than anything else. For a moment, it looked as though they were in trouble. It was then that Frank George remembered an old contact in the Eastern part of the city who had a workshop.

They took off, not knowing if he was still there, and unsure of the reaction they would get to such a request.

Fortunately, he was still there. However, a problem arose when the duo realized that neither could speak more than just a few words of German, and the engineer no more than a few of English. Not to be thwarted at this stage, Bert proceeded to tell his new European friend exactly what they needed to make this gas-firing gun.

> He must have been about 70, this old bloke, and looked totally un-bothered with us arriving there. He twigged straight away as to what we wanted from my rather awful sign-language and sketches. He wouldn't let us help, mind, but had it ready in two days. We were amazed.
>
> We took it on set, and rigged all the pipes up the legs and down the sleeve and so on and it worked a treat. The director was rather pleased with us that day!

The event engraved on Bert's mind was witnessing young couples actual escape attempt across the Wall.

> They were shot, there and then. It was awful and brutal. I'll never ever forget that. It was such a waste of life, and so cold.
>
> Looking up the scene, really, for the first time, hit home: all of the towers with armed guards, the barbed wire on the wall, the searchlights. It was like something from a prisoner of war film. But this was no film. To the guards involved in the shooting, it just seemed like an everyday thing. That was the worst thing about it.

Soon after completing the film, Harry Saltzman gave Bert and Frank George two copies of a book entitled *Cold War in a Country Garden* which he was planning to turn into a feature film. They were immediately captivated with the story, and set about thinking how they'd approach the effects.

> I think it was absolutely fascinating. It never came off, however, proba-bly for reasons of finance, and although the idea has been used in films of recent times, it was—to my knowledge—the first time a project of that sort and scope had been muted.
>
> It was all about the future population explosion and how there just wouldn't be enough room on the earth for everyone to live, so a group of government-funded scientists initiated a "shrinking" research pro-

gram. Basically, they wanted to shrink people to one and a half inches to make more room in the world.

One particular group of volunteers were shrunk in size and put back in their own garden, to see how they would survive. Of course, little things like ants and spiders were absolute giants to them, and blades of grass would have been the equivalent to six foot high.

In those days, there were no computers and they really would have had to build sets ten times bigger than normal to create the vastness of the surroundings. Frank and I were bursting with ideas, but alas didn't get the chance to realize any of them. I really regret that.

Back to the Skies

Bert did work again with Harry Saltzman on the epic *Battle of Britain* (1969), telling the story of Britain's dramatic 1940 battle of the air against the Luftwaffe. Guy Hamilton again took the helm of an all-star vehicle: Laurence Olivier, Robert Shaw, Michael Caine, Christopher Plummer, Kenneth More, Susannah York, Trevor Howard, Ralph Richardson ... the list goes on. Amazingly, despite the heavyweight cast and excellent action, the film lost some $10 million.

The principal special effects man on the picture was Wally Vevas, although Cliff Richardson had quite a big involvement too. Wally asked Frank George and me to work with him on the picture during pre-production because, he said, he knew I was ex–RAF and hence have a good understanding of what we were dealing with. At that time though, I was engaged on a *Carry On* picture (Up the Jungle) and so the studio—who still employed me—couldn't accept his offer.

After five or six weeks, my *Carry On* stint came to an end and I became available. Wally grabbed me and said, "Will you come on *Battle of Britain* now?" Needless to say, I jumped at it.

Wally was a lovely chap to work with, but much more electrically and mechanically minded than I was. Whereas I'd pull it with a piece of string, as per my mentor Frank George's training, he was one of the sort who'd have six electric motors on it, if you know what I mean. A prime example came with the model work.

We had hundreds of models: Spitfires, Hurricanes ... you name it, we had it. They literally made them by the hundred, all out of brass and with about a five-inch wing span.

I remember 1940 well, and recall the hundreds of planes that filled the sky flying into battle. That's what we had to recreate on E-stage. Wally had lines and lines of wires across the stage against a blue screen, with squadron after squadron after squadron of model planes on the wires moving across the stage; all pulled by motors. As any old film hand will tell you, it is very rare to capture a complicated sequence like this on the first take, and so you prepare for multiple takes. Wally, however, hadn't as he had no means of rewinding the planes back across the stage. He had all these planes stuck at one end of the stage.

Incidentally, the planes were made of brass because it was the ideal weight to keep the models stable. Aluminum would have been too light to move effectively and realistically.

They later got it all working, and in post-production superimposed the clouds and so on over the blue screen and it looked damn good in the film, especially with the sound effects dubbed on. It brought back some fairly scary memories of 1940, I can tell you.

Larger models (almost life-size) of the Spitfires were manufactured in Pinewood's plasterer's shop for use on the airstrips, as the producers couldn't secure (nor afford) enough real Spitfires. Dozens poured out of the shop and onto transporters. It was quite a sight to behold.

Telemark

On the other side of the lot, Kirk Douglas and Richard Harris had joined forces with director Anthony Mann for an ice-set action adventure called *The Heroes of Telemark*. Their arguments were widely reported and legendary. But that's another story. Bert was approached by the director of effects, Ronnie Ballinger, to make a model of an armored car that was to be smashed in the opening sequence. Pretty easy one, might think. Well, the size of the model was to be comparable with a Mini car. Not a typical miniature by any means.

The armored car was supposed to be hit by a big boulder that was pushed down the hill by the resistance fighters, and in going over the edge of the road, and cliff, exploded.

The boulder was pretty lightweight, because there were actors involved, so they couldn't do it "for real." They needed a convincing model that could be knocked off the road by the boulder. Ronnie said we had about three months to make a complete replica.

It really was as big as a small car and they took it out to the paddock tank at Pinewood, not out to Telemark, thank God, where it was ten below zero! There they proceeded to send it off a "cliff" and destroy it by setting off the charges I'd put inside it. I really hate seeing my hard work broken into a hundred pieces like that, as one takes great pride in it, but there you are; it was needed for a reason, and that was the reason. Mind you, it cost about £2,000 — then — which would have bought a damn nice car.

The Chairman

Hijinks and action followed again, this time in North Wales, when Bert took up an assignment on J. Lee Thompson's *The Most Dangerous Man in the World* (a.k.a. *The Chairman*). Gregory Peck starred as an idealist scientist recruited to infiltrate Chairman Mao's inner sanctum, after first having a small chip and transmitter implanted in his head. What he does know is that it was also a bomb which could be detonated at any time.

Most of the Chinese mountain scenes were filmed in Snowdonia, in absolutely awful weather, as Bert recalled:

The rains were torrential over the majority of the daylight hours — it always stopped at night, of course — and at the front of Snowdon, in the shadow of the oncoming Chinese army, we rigged up barbed wire fences and I had to plant explosives in the ground to represent the shells landing.

I dug several holes over about a hundred yards before returning to go back to the first to plant the charges, by which time it was full of water. As fast as I could dig them, they filled up with rain water. It was terrible. Poor old Greg and the rest of the crew had to film their scenes in all this too. My bombs, which were about eight inches in diameter, were floating in the peat-sodden holes, but somehow I managed to make them all work.

By the end of the day, we were all absolutely soaked from top to bottom. Yet, amazingly, spirits remained high. I know that Greg hated it up there, but he never really let it show, either with us or on-screen.

The next morning we went out to see what damage there was as, obviously, after detonating explosives in the ground, one has to insure that all is okay and the ground is level again before leaving. That's part of the job — going out and tidying up, and usually when everyone else has gone home. It didn't take long.

Back in London, Bert's mother had been taken seriously ill and passed away while he was on location, miles away from anywhere. Director J. Lee Thompson immediately allowed Bert to return home to his family. Although the circumstances of his return were immensely sad, Bert was in fact mightily relieved to leave the awful location.

Nessie

Legendary director Billy Wilder took up residence at Pinewood to film *The Private Life of Sherlock Holmes* (1969). A stellar cast included Robert Stephens, Colin Blakely (as Holmes and Watson), Genevieve Page, Clive Revell, Christopher Lee and Stanley Holloway. It was a very ambitious and personal project for Wilder, one which resulted in some very good reviews (but poor box office returns).

A complete recreation of Victorian Baker Street (built on the studio's back lot) was designed by Alex Trauner, and cost some £80,000. The cobbled street consisted of real cobbles, each house had a real cellar and the materials were extremely good quality. Trauner did come in for some criticism for creating some practical problems (involving projection techniques) and was called a "builder of houses, not sets" by director of photography Christopher Challis.

> The film was very placid in terms of effects, but I was brought in for some stage work, and primarily to flood the Baker Street set with the thick London smog of the day — I used smoke pots, in fact. The film involved Holmes on the trail of the Loch Ness Monster and the whole unit went on location to Loch Ness in Scotland, where again I was asked to supply the mist on the Loch. In reality there is very rarely thick mist over the Loch day and night, but that's what they wanted.
>
> Sightings of the Monster, or Nessie as she is known, are stuff of legends. Numerous people claim to have seen her, and photographs have been produced, most of which were dismissed as fakes. I don't disbelieve the existence of a monster, but I've yet to be convinced.
>
> Wally Vevas made a model Nessie which they wanted to use in the film, and rather good it was too. She was lowered into the Loch and was probably about 40 foot in length and, typical of the ideas of what Nessie looked like, had numerous humps and the like, and similar to a very large eel of sorts. She was to be towed across the Loch by a little tugboat.
>
> My colleague Jim Harris and I armed ourselves with the big old smoke machines and rowed out onto the Loch on a raft, which was no great pleasure for me, let me tell you. Obviously we needed to be a fair distance away so as to be out of shot. There we sat and watched the monster being towed across time and time again, still pumping our smoke out. As smoke doesn't always do what you want, because the wind often picks up and blows it in totally the opposite direction, it involves a lot of waiting for the right conditions. Finally we got the okay and our smoke moved across the water beautifully. Billy Wilder called "action" and the tug started pulling the monster. However, it

reached a point a few hundred yards in, and the monster started getting lower and lower in the water. The top half then went under, then the middle part and then the whole damn lot. The tug started struggling and we realized that it was obviously being pulled down too.

The captain ran out of the cabin and, taking an axe, cut through the rope. The monster sank without trace and was never seen again whilst the tug regained control of itself.

Jim and I sat and watched. Almost in total disbelief.

It was a very convincing monster, with scales and very precise details, and poor old Wally was terribly disappointed that his work had sank to the dark depths of Loch Ness—and it is dark down there because it's all peat soil around and below. You really can't see your hand in front of your face in that water. I know that because a group of research students were up there at the same time as us, and they had a wonderful bright yellow two-man submarine. We used to have a natter and after our monster sank, I asked them to look out for it when they were next down and to see if they could snag a line on her. They said it'd be like looking for a needle in a haystack, as the Loch is miles in length and very, very deep and very dark. Many was the time they got lost down there, in fact.

I've often wondered what might happen if the monster did resurface one day. It would cause quite a stir, I would imagine, and I'd have a little chuckle to myself during it all.

Mummy

Around this time, Bert was approached to join a production of a Sexton Blake episode. Sadly, his memory of the personnel involved is a little sketchy—but with over 100 credits under his belt, that can't be surprising.

It wasn't something I'd have immediately associated with Blake, as it was set in Egypt and concerned with all the old Egyptology and mummy stuff.

Although I'd seen old films with mummies and so forth, it wasn't a subject I was too familiar with. What did a Mummy actually look like close up, and how was it preserved? What were its surroundings in its tomb? They were questions to which I didn't know the answers. So off I trotted to a few London museums.

Unfortunately, most museums won't let you take photographs and so I took my sketch pad along and made quite a few drawings, to the best of my ability. Then came the hieroglyphics. Each tomb has hieroglyphics unique to the particular person entombed, I learned, and I set about

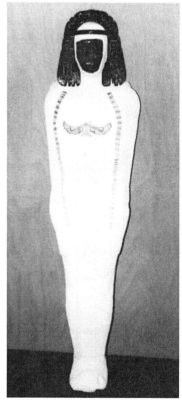

Left: Sexton Blake's "Mummy" with Bert. *Right:* The "Mummy" alone.

copying a few — the easiest ones, to be honest. I knew it didn't matter too much about getting the detail spot on, as long as it didn't look out of place in the film.

Back at the studio, I amassed my research material, and starting making the mummy. Not an easy task, as anyone who has ever attempted it will tell you. I started off with a mannequin and a whole load of plaster bandages, which I was quite adept with using after my St. John's Ambulance training. Then I had to complete the designs on the chest, which all mummies had — a sort of insignia.

Bert's second task was to make a gold shield approximately three foot by two and a half foot, and which had to "explode into a thousand pieces," according to the script.

I obviously realized that I couldn't use anything like Fiberglas, as that would never explode into tiny little pieces as required. So I decided to use breakaway glass. I designed a mold for the plaster department, and from it they made two shields for us. They went off to the paint shop for a covering of paint, and I then attached something like 20 tiny detonators to the first shield; the second was held in reserve, connected by hair-thin wires which would disintegrate upon explosion, and no trace would be left for the camera to pick up. I'd never tried anything like it before, so was unsure as to whether it would work. I'm pleased to say it worked perfectly and the golden shield did just as the script instructed. Quite a few people were curious as to how I'd done it, but I never let on ... until now.

Dad's Army

The popular and endearing BBC comedy series received the big screen treatment in 1971 after many successful seasons on the small screen. The storyline concerned the misadventures of a fictitious seaside town of Walmington on Sea and its Home Guard platoon during World War II. The elderly collection of gents in uniform included Arthur Lowe, John LeMesurier, John Laurie, Clive Dunn and Ian Lavender.

> I'll forever remember dear John Laurie, who was an accomplished Scottish actor having appeared in many acclaimed stage roles prior to a successful film career, saying to the writers Jimmy Perry and David Croft, "I've been acting for near on 40 years, yet I have to wait to appear in this crap to become famous."
> He meant it in a nice way, but it was ever so funny!
> My involvement in *Dad's Army* was principally in a barn sequence. In it there were loads and loads of sacks of grain and one of the platoon was to accidentally catch a sack with a bayonet and hey presto that sack, and all of the others too, poured their contents all over the troops—and they did pour real grain too, on cue to my detonation.

Persuading

In 1971, Bert worked on his first major TV series at Pinewood, *The Persuaders*. The show starred Roger Moore and Tony Curtis as a suave sophisticated English playboy aristocrat and a rough-edged New York wheeler dealer, respectively; the duo teamed in adventures of intrigue, wrongdoing and general mayhem.

After his massive seven-year success as TV's *The Saint*, Roger Moore vowed never to return to TV, preferring instead to concentrate on his

Roger Moore, Lew Grade and Tony Curtis during *The Persuaders.*

movie career. When TV mogul Lew Grade initially offered him the series, Moore declined. At least, initially. Grade — ever the persuasive salesman — explained that he had already sold the series to American TV with him and Tony Curtis, and offered Moore a rather large paycheck. He then appealed to Moore's patriotic side by saying that "England needs the money. And think about your Queen." Moore signed, and a 24-part series was set up with Moore's longtime collaborator Bob Baker producing. Moore, incidentally, directed several episodes of the show as well as dressing up in drag for one episode.

Both Roger and Tony were smashing to work with, and so much fun. The show was played pretty much tongue-in-cheek, as you might expect with them two. There weren't many major effects as such, but I was on constant call as the odd thing would crop up that I'd have to attend to on the spot.

"Hang around, Bert, we might need you" was the line I always got. They liked to have me around if (say) someone was due to get a dunking in water, or a gun was involved. In fact, I remember a director calling me over one day and saying how he wanted a bullet fired through a door — just like that.

It was in the Green Room of the main Pinewood mansion, actually, and so I asked him what the door was made of — knowing it was very expensive oak. He said that he thought it was oak or something. Yes, I replied, and how much would you say it is worth?

He estimated a couple of hundred pounds. Fine, said I, and went on to explain about how I would need to totally destroy it. His arms shot up in the air and he said I couldn't possibly do that.

I asked how he expected me to do it. He then suggested the door was changed to one made of less expensive material that I could destroy. The very next day, I set my charge inside the "fake" door and did the scene.

It was very much a day-by-day, week-by-week assignment for me with the aforementioned odd explosion, a few guns, smashing of glass and, as such, a very pleasant mix and not too demanding nor taxing.

Sleuth

Bert's next feature reunited him with his design mentor Ken Adam, who had designed the production for the Michael Caine–Laurence Olivier two-hander *Sleuth*. The film was shot mainly on one set at Pinewood — one which had to lend itself to all of the movement and demands of the script. It was, again, a very agreeable assignment for Bert as he had to travel all of 300 yards from his workshop to the stage.

It was quite a complex shoot, and quite intense. The schedule and planning proved to be rather erratic for Bert as he was never sure what would happen from day to day as there was a fair amount of improvisation. It was unusual for a film in terms of stage effects; everything was very last-minute, and it was not the way Bert liked to work. Planning and preparation were everything to him. He did, however, enjoy working with Ken Adam and Michael Caine again, and often marveled at the brilliance and wonderfully strong screen presence of Olivier.

Travels

TV beckoned once again with a brief stint on Peter Hunt's version of *Gulliver's Travels*, most of which was shot on the special effects stage at Pinewood.

Contrary to what you might think, there weren't many models or miniatures used in the production, but we did have a great many "small" actors and scaled everything accordingly with special photographic processes; that's another way of achieving a desired effect, and perhaps a less expensive one to using giant sets in the first instance.

Panther

When Blake Edwards made the first *Pink Panther* film, he catapulted Peter Sellers to international star status. Although Sellers had made many other films, TV and radio programs it was turning him into a bumbling French detective that proved the stroke of genius. Having made two, *The*

Peter Sellers immortalized as Inspector Clouseau at Pinewood Studios.

Pink Panther and *A Shot in the Dark*, Sellers left Inspector Clouseau behind to pursue other roles. However, perhaps to help raise his profile once again after a number of less-than-successful films, he returned to work with Edwards on *Return of the Pink Panther* (1974).

The supporting cast included Christopher Plummer as Sir Charles Litton a.k.a. the notorious Phantom; Herbert Lom as an increasingly insane Chief Inspector Dreyfuss, intent on killing Clouseau; and Burt Kwouk as Clouseau's faithful — and karate chopping — manservant Cato.

I went to Shepperton Studios with that one, if memory serves me correctly, just a half hour away from Pinewood.

There was a wonderful sequence in the film — my favorite, in fact — with Clouseau dressed as an hysterically ridiculous telephone engineer character. He wanted to put a bug on Litton's phone line, as he suspected him of being the Phantom, who had recently stolen the priceless Pink Panther diamond.

A great comedy routine ensued with Clouseau ringing the doorbell and busting it, and then, once having gained entry, creating chaos in trying to put the tap on the phone. A tube of super glue features, and you couldn't imagine the chaos one tiny tube of that can cause!

One of the little gags that Blake wanted in the room was a table lamp in which the bulb kept popping up, and literally jumped into the air. Each time Clouseau had to catch it — whilst trying hard to do something else at the same time. It was so funny.

It was a simple enough gimmick, actually, as it was just a spring-loaded lamp base in which the bulb sat, and when I pressed the trigger, it clicked, the spring was engaged and up came the bulb. I obviously had to do it on cue, and it was quite tricky actually as there was lots going on in that scene and I had to get it just right.

Blake Edwards was very much the perfectionist, as indeed was Peter, and whilst being very polite I must admit he wasn't quite in the same mold as Gerry Thomas from the *Carry Ons*. He was a bit more harsh and terse at times. When I later did a few days on *Victor Victoria*, I thought he was a bit sharp with his wife Julie Andrews in directing her. But he got the results, you see. Different directors have different methods of working, I guess I just wasn't used to his. Maybe had I done a few more pictures with him, I would have been.

I recently met up again with Burt Kwouk, who hasn't changed a bit, and asked him if he ever got hurt in the films as he and Peter used to knock seven bells out of each other on screen. To my great surprise, he said he never so much as scratched himself. I shouldn't be surprised, really, as being in the business I know I plan everything in my job meticulously, as would the fight choreographers on the *Panthers*. But in watching some of the Cato-Clouseau fights, I often find myself feeling the pain of the punches, throws and door slammings.

The Sex Shop

Back at Pinewood, the strange requests still came in.

I was asked if I could make some lances for a medieval jousting film. The instructions were a bit more precise than that, as the lances had to be seen to penetrate and release blood. It wasn't a problem as, in fact, it was just a larger version of the blood knife which has a spring-loaded end, which in turn goes inside the main body of the blade rather than the "victim."

I had to make six of these lances, and realized that I would need rather large bulbs to house the fake blood; such that when the actor squeezed a certain part of the handle (as he pushed the tip of the lance "into" another actor, as though stabbing him), blood would be released through the tip.

I couldn't really think of where I could get any extra large rubber bulbs. After a while, I decided to follow up

Retractable knife and a "hot" knife. (Robin Harbour.)

on a hunch I'd had. I ventured into Slough to a shop which was, well, what might nowadays be called a "sex shop." I'd never been into one of these places before and wasn't sure what to expect. Needless to say, I soon developed a name for myself there, too.

I asked the man behind the counter if he had any large enema bulbs. He said he had, and passed me one. It looked like just what I'd envisaged.

"Smashing," I said. "I'll take six."

"Six?"

"Yes, six," I reiterated.

"Are you expecting trouble, sir?" asked the disbelieving man.

I didn't even bother attempting to explain, as he wouldn't have believed me.

My hunch paid off, though, as the lances worked beautifully.

Scene Eight

A Little Bit of Horror

Dracula Has Risen from the Grave (1968) was the first time the evil Count (Christopher Lee) ventured away from Hammer's traditional home at Bray Studios and set up shop at Pinewood. Acclaimed (and Oscar-winning) cinematographer Freddie Francis helmed the picture — and developed something of a name for himself as a director in the horror genre.

"You just can't keep a good man down!" was the poster tag-line. The film, upon its release, came in for a certain amount of criticism for being tedious, confined and repetitive. The subject matter and its potential box-office success or failure isn't an issue that technicians like Bert become involved with. They are just happy to see another film move into production, and to benefit from the work generated. Of course, they serve the project with the utmost professionalism and dedication and always hope it will do well; that is to everyone's long-term benefit. Many are remembered and hailed, but then again, there are the odd few best forgotten too.

> The Hammer films are generally grouped as being horror, but to be honest, nowadays children laugh at them; they're not that horrific, at least not by today's standards. Perhaps that says something about standards nowadays? But let's not get into that one.

Dissolving

> On *Dracula*, my principal job, under Jimmy Snow who was director of effects, was to set up the scene where Chris Lee is impaled on a large crucifix at the end of the film.

That scene is a perfect example of how the various departments work together on an effect.

Chris "fell" onto the crucifix and was, according to the script, to "disintegrate."

We had a dummy for the impaling part, and took shots of Chris in the buildup to it. From there we had to use dummies in various states of disintegration: enter the makeup, prop and camera departments.

The cameraman had to make sure his set-up didn't move throughout the creation of the sequence. It was basically a case of time-lapse photography and dissolves, as we switched the dummy — ending up with just a pile of ash.

Christopher Lee

I guess you could say the effects were more photographic than "special" but they had to be coordinated all the same.

In the final print, perhaps for timing reasons, the scene was shortened, cutting out the disintegration sequence. It became a direct cut from Dracula impaled on the crucifix to the other characters, and then back to just a crucifix, minus Dracula.

We were also asked to design and build a large vampire bat for a sequence where Dracula was going to transform into one to make good his escape from a tight corner. That was fun. Of course, it had to look realistic and quite large, whilst being able to be "flown" using wires. It was good experience for the eagles I had to make later in my career for Hertz, but more about that later.

Again, that sequence was not used in the final version of the film so, while Bert's input was significant, none is evident in the print as it stands.

Vampire bat

Ingrid Pitt and Nigel Green

A couple of years later, Bert was engaged to work on another Hammer picture, *Countess Dracula*, starring Ingrid Pitt in the title role and Nigel Green.

Pitt has since developed something of a following as a star of horror films and has lately written two books on the genre. In her career she appeared in David Lean's *Dr. Zhivago* and *A Funny Thing Happened on the Way to the Forum* in minor roles, but received her big break with *Where Eagles Dare* (1968), starring Clint Eastwood and Richard Burton. From there she joined the Hammer stable for *The Vampire Lovers.*

> Ingrid was a charming lady and quite the opposite to her character in the film, I'm pleased to say. What really amazed me with her was her sheer tenacity and determination to succeed. I later discovered that she had endured awful experiences at the hands of the Nazis in concentration camps that she and her mother were held in. Words cannot describe what she went through, and I admired her, and admire her still, tremendously for it.

Nigel Green was a stalwart of British film and TV. His credits ranged from *Zulu* to *Khartoum*, *The Ipcress File*, *Jason and the Argonauts* and some of the *Fu Manchu* films. Bert went on to work with him again on Green's final film *Gawain and the Green Knight* (1972), made shortly before he died from an overdose of sleeping pills.

Nigel was an absolutely charming chap. In *Countess Dracula* I remember him having a rather large dagger which was attached to his belt, dangling over his groin. It was a bloody heavy dagger, and when he moved it obviously moved — over his groin area. Needless to say, it became quite uncomfortable.

The director Peter Sasdy asked if I could do anything to help make things more comfortable for Nigel. I suggested that I could make a Fiberglas replica, and in fact, I did. Three were made in the end, and they were a lot lighter to handle. Nigel's eyes didn't water quite so much after I'd substituted my replica for the real thing — which, as a matter of fact, I still own.

Pins

There were several rather unpleasant scenes for Ingrid to get to grips with in the film, and rather uncomfortable too — for both of us. One of which was when she had to pierce a girl's throat with a six-inch pin — I think you would call it a hat pin, in fact.

It was the first time I'd ever had to deal with a retractable weapon on this small scale, and didn't relish the idea. It was very tricky to work on, if I'm honest.

I took a hypodermic syringe, a horse's one — and they don't like it up 'em either — from a local vet. I cut it down and blunted the end. Next I made a pin to insert into the end of it. Obviously, when you're talking about making a thing which could prove extremely dangerous if it went wrong, then it becomes quite worrying. Therefore, a very blunt pin went into the end of the syringe, but I soon realized that it would be impossible to make it retractable; as I could never have found or made a spring small enough to sit behind the pin. It only had a diameter of a couple of millimeters at the most.

I explained all this to Peter Sasdy, and he was quite marvelous about it and said he'd work around it with the cameraman. What we agreed on was that as long as the pin was retractable when it went into the girl's throat, then they'd film that part before tackling the withdrawal of it, which was filmed in reverse to create the illusion of it penetrating and then being pulled out. So in fact we "penetrated" twice and just reversed one of the shots, and it made life a lot easier all round.

It worked brilliantly, too, as you'll see in the film!

Blood

Sasdy had one more request regarding the scene. He wanted blood to squirt out from the actress' neck into the camera. Unfazed, Bert said he could arrange it.

One thing Peter didn't realize was that someone would have to pump the blood through a little tube I'd put together, with a glorified bicycle pump, if it was going to look realistic, and really squirt as he envisaged. It was a prop man who landed the task, if my memory serves me.

He was a very capable chap, but perhaps a little overenthusiastic as the end of the tube came off the pump with the sheer force of his pressure on it, and blood went everywhere. And I mean everywhere — most of the crew, and me, were covered in it.

It wasn't regarded as one of Peter's better ideas, shall we shall.

The film's premise involved Ingrid Pitt's titular Hungarian noblewoman, bathing in the blood of young virgins to restore her youth. Bert was charged with organizing it despite his protests of already having had a bath that week.

I wouldn't say I used virgin's blood — there weren't many around, to be honest! I made up some stage blood, but thickened it up a bit more for effect. It couldn't have been particularly pleasant for Ingrid to have to get into this horrible gooey red stuff, let alone be naked and doing it.

It was very much a closed set that day, and I was probably one of the only people allowed to get close to Ingrid. I dare say she thought I was only involved in the scene so as I might get a good look at her, and she asked if I'd ever done it before. Tongue-in-cheek, I said I had. Well, I wasn't strictly lying as I have been involved with the St. John's Ambulance Service for many years, and got to see quite a few things in strange situations. It was, though, a job to me, and it didn't really register, nor matter that I was working with a nude actress. I know it's a bit of a novelty for some of the more immature crew members, and they giggle and joke about it, but believe me it isn't particularly erotic standing in the middle of a film set, with scores of lights on you, cameras setting-up and 40 crew waiting to get on with the scene. Of that you can be sure.

It was a very happy film for Bert, apart from the odd gruesome effect that was called for, and he got along famously with Pitt, Sasdy and Green — whom Bert maintains was a much underrated actor and one never really stretched with his film material.

Scene from *Twins of Evil.*

Double Trouble

The following year, 1971, a young director named John Hough turned his hand to another Hammer offering, *Twins of Evil*. It starred Mary and Madeleine Collinson as identical Austrian twins who become involved with a vampire cult, with Peter Cushing and Dennis Price in support. Another typical Hammer bloodfest.

That was another completely different kettle of fish. By this time I had graduated to being a fully fledged effects man, in charge of such matters on the film.

Peter Cushing was an absolutely charming and courteous gentleman. I will never hear a word said against him. Although he had such a marvelously gaunt face that suited these type of films, he was by far the most gentle of people you could ever have met.

One of the scenes I had to work on with Peter was a decapitation of one of the twins. I asked if Peter would be doing it on film, and he said, to my great surprise, "No, you're doing it." Charming.

I sat and thought long and hard about how I was going to do it. It had to look realistic, and also have blood pumping out all over the place, naturally. Obviously, I could use a blood knife, or rather, machete which would pump out a certain amount of the old red stuff, but if you've ever seen a decapitation you'll know there's a heck of a lot of blood pumped out of the jugular, so I needed to make a new neck for the victim that I could shoot blood out of. Initially, I decided to use a huge piece of Spam, but that didn't work.

The meat wasn't wasted however, as Bert took it home where he and his family made good use of it for their evening meal.

Next I tried — at the suggestion of the director — a marrow. We had to have two pipes channeling the blood through the neck, and the marrow just didn't support them effectively. I tried one or two other things, to no avail, before I picked up a huge sausage from the butchers — it was a German one, and about four inches in diameter. I bought two of them, as always, and we had a good meal of that (unused) second one!

John Hough was adamant that I should perform the severing of the

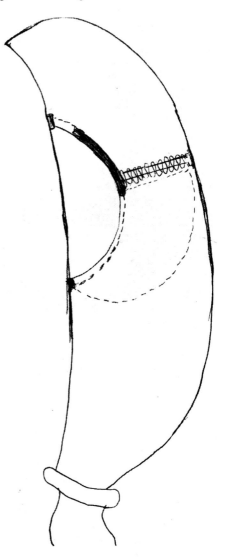

The Twins of Evil machete design.

head. I told him that the only way I'd do it is if he shot half of it in reverse, limiting any potential danger to the actress. I put the machete to her neck and pulled it away; they shot it backwards so it looked like I was actually swinging it in to the neck. For the next half of the shot, I substituted my sausage for the neck.

We had a little man who was about 4 foot high, dressed in the girl's costume, with this huge sausage on his head! I then laid into the meat and the machete came away with blood gushing everywhere. If you see the film, it is my hand in Peter Cushing's glove. It wasn't an easy scene, nor particularly satisfactory from my point of view, but it served its purpose.

A disintegration scene was also included, and similar techniques to those used in *Dracula Has Risen from the Grave* were employed — old hat to Bert!

More Theatrics

An all-star cast highlighted Bert's next horror picture, *Theater of Blood*. Vincent Price, Diana Rigg, Ian Hendry, Harry Andrews, Coral Browne, Jack Hawkins, Diana Dors, Dennis Price, Arthur Lowe and Eric Sykes were just a few of the names in the cast list, and Bert was certainly keeping distinguished company.

Coral Browne, it must be said, was regarded as something of a maneater. Legend has it that when she arrived on set for the first time, she spotted a young man amongst the crew and said to her accompanying friend, "I'm going to have him." Her friend knew this particular man to be gay, and so said, "I very much doubt it, dear." Coral immediately made a bet of £1 (20 shillings) that she would indeed "have" him that night.

The next day, Coral arrived on set and said to her friend, "You owe me 10 shillings"!

The film company hired an actual film theater in Putney, southwest London. The story involved Vincent as a Shakespearean actor who took murderous revenge on his critics, and so this was a very suitable location. The theater was actually due to be demolished, and as we needed to gut it with a fire later on, it suited all parties for us to use it.

I had met and worked with Vincent on several films prior to this. Like Peter Cushing, he was delightful man. He was also a wonderful cook.

Diana Rigg was interesting to work with. Whilst I got along with her fine, she was a bit "cold" at times — a little like my experiences of

Patrick McGoohan — and so the friendship never really developed beyond the necessary exchanges between us on set.

Heads Will Roll

One of the scenes involved Vincent getting rid of Arthur Lowe by cutting off his head, in bed. For this particular disposal, Arthur had to have a full head cast made. This, I assure you, is not a pleasant thing for anyone. He came up to Pinewood and we sat him in a chair with two straws up his nose, to enable him to breathe and then the plaster of Paris went on. It took hours, and during it Arthur couldn't see anything, nor hear much — he just had his straws.

We finally made the false head for the shot, and it worked wonderfully well. When Arthur was shaken to wake him in his bed in the morning, off rolled the head! I did in fact have this false head in my workshop for some years, but when I retired it was along with Ozzie and a lot of other stuff, disposed of.

Arthur became a very good friend of mine. He was a placid and mild-mannered person, and totally the opposite to the pompous Capt. Mainwaring in *Dad's Army*. I miss him dearly.

The grand finale called for the theater to be set on fire. John Stears and Bert arranged for the entire interior to go up in flames ahead of the building's demolition. Within a couple of days of completing filming inside, it was flattened.

Zombies

My next horror picture was over at Twickenham Studios. Again, it was with Vincent Price and the shooting title was *March of the Zombies*.

It also featured another damn fire too. For this one, I had to set fire to a whole set inside the stage. It was a big old set, and mainly built out of plastic boarding, because they couldn't afford anything else.

In those days we used a thing called petroleum jelly to get fires going, as I've already mentioned with the *Firechasers* story, and I knew full well that had I put jelly on this set it would have gone up in flames in about two minutes. That's what they wanted though, they said.

I agreed to do it, and asked them to switch off the smoke alarms and have the fire people outside the stage with hoses ready. To my great surprise and amazement, I was informed that they hadn't even planned to use a fire department to put out the flames. They hummed and harred a bit about the expense, before a cocky second assistant came over and said, "You have four minutes to do it."

Hang on, I said, I'll do it when I am satisfied it is safe to do it — and I'm not. He started arguing with me and dear old Vincent overheard, and came over.

"You there," he said to the A.D. "Are you in charge of the special effects on this film?"

"No."

"Exactly," said Vincent. "He is," and he pointed at me. "You will do exactly what Bert says and without argument. Do I make myself clear? Because I am going to be on that set when it goes up."

He was going to be on the set, as his character was going to be the one who set fire to it all. When we were eventually ready, Vincent made a point of checking I was happy and that the fire brigade were outside and ready. He then gave me the okay.

I'd tarred the whole place down with jelly solution and Vincent went along and set fire to it all. There weren't any problems, it went like clockwork, and a few minutes later the fire brigade were in extinguishing it all. It was a very simple sequence to arrange, but all the hassle came in fighting to make sure adequate safety precautions were taken!

Bert does not suffer fools gladly when safety issues are involved, because he knows too well that lives are at stake in sequences that involve fires. Handled correctly, with the right planning, these sort of sequences can be extremely simple and straightforward. Handled badly, by inexperienced people, they can lead to disaster.

All that some people are concerned about is what shows on screen, no matter what has to be done to get it on screen. All that I am concerned about is what happens off the screen and thankfully I've never hurt anyone in an effect, and that is my proudest achievement. Health and safety is much hotter in the business now too. God, I remember climbing a ladder with two sticks of dynamite in my top pocket and two detonators in my back one. That would never be allowed today and I don't think I'd want to do it either.

Of course, nowadays in these types of films, computers can come in and take away the most dangerous elements — which is good. Mind, the flip side of that is that people coming into the business don't know how to achieve and handle these sequences without using those computers. I'm not so sure that's a good thing. Computers should be used as tools as and when appropriate, sure, but not all of the time and for everything as some people think they should. It's like calculators in school, for example. Kids know how to use them to solve problems but do they know about the processes which the calculators use? I also argue that the expense involved in using computers could sometimes be better utilized in practical effects, which are, of course, better as they actually happen there and then, not on some screen in Soho. More on all that a little later.

Touched

The Medusa Touch, a film based on the novel by Peter Van Greenaway, starred Richard Burton, Lino Ventura, Lee Remick and Harry Andrews. Whilst not perhaps a horror film in the vein of Hammer, the film could easily compete in the "scary" scorings.

The film was produced by Anne V. Coates, who is J. Arthur Rank's niece and a rather famous editor. The story was all about how Burton's character believes he can create disasters. And there are quite a few in the film, climaxing when a London cathedral caves in.

That was a strange story, actually, and right at the beginning I was asked to work on the effects throughout the production. But a few weeks into the schedule I was informed, very nicely, that I had "been relieved of duties" on the picture. I couldn't understand it, to be honest, but then learned that the production had secured another effects man cheaper than me! Marvelous, eh? In my few weeks I worked closely with the makeup people in creating some lovely stuff like boils, big blisters and the like that bubbled up on people's faces.

I think it was the first and only time I had been asked to leave a picture before it had finished. It didn't particularly worry me, but made me think.

SCENE NINE

Television Beckons

"Without Bert Luxford, we never could have had the Q series."
— Spike Milligan

In the mid–1970s, Bert left Pinewood's employ to become a freelance special effects technician. In doing so, he joined the board of Effects Associates, also a Pinewood-based company.

Bert then found himself sub-contracted to several different companies, one of which was the BBC.

Service please

The first show I worked on for them was *Are You Being Served?*, which was great fun and the characters were absolutely great.

The long-running series which first hit television screens in 1972 was the brainchild of David Croft and Jeremy Lloyd, and followed the misadventures of the clothing department staff of a large (fictitious) London department store, Grace Brothers. It spawned two follow-up series, one set in Australia and the other, *Grace and Favor* (1992), after the death of Young Mr. Grace, their employer. There was also a feature film outing set in the fictional holiday resort the Costa Plonka in Portugal during a store refurbishment.

The regular cast included Mollie Sugden as Mrs. Mary Elizabeth "Betty" Jennifer Rachel Yiddell Abergavenny Slocombe, John Inman as Wilberforce Clayborne Humphries, Frank Thornton as Capt. Stephen Peacock, Wendy Richard as Miss Shirley Brahms, Nicholas Smith as Cuthbert Rumbold and Harold Bennet as Young Mr. Grace.

John Inman

What names, eh?! I had quite a lot to do with the series. You'll recall the many counter top display units that were brought onto the shop floor — everything from spinning bow ties and inflatable bras to revolving bowler hats ... all terribly funny. For one particular episode, I was asked to make an illuminated suit for John Inman, who played the very camp Mr. Humphries in the show. It was a pain in the back of the neck because it had something like 90 LEDs [similar to small bulbs] in it, and they all had to be sewn in and wired up.

I went out to a local electronics shop and asked for a hundred LEDs. The chap behind the counter asked me if I was starting up a factory, and said no, I wanted them for a suit. Needless to say, he looked at me as though I was stark raving mad. But I was getting used to that.

He couldn't manage a hundred there and then, but came up with about 60 and promised I could have the rest another day. Great, I said, I can make a start on the suit. He still didn't believe what I was going to do.

Anyway, the wardrobe department at the BBC made a suit out of a reflective blue material — with a hat to match too — and I took it away for a colleague, Doug Winter, and me to put the lights in. It took us about three days, as we not only had to stitch the wiring and LEDs in, we then had to put the lining in too; that was important because we didn't want John to catch a wire when he was putting his arm into the sleeve. Doug's wife was, fortunately, a seamstress and worked with us on it for a while. Meanwhile, Doug's son came up with the pocket-sized power pack, which was just like a few ordinary batteries stuck together actually, and I think it was the first time I'd ever been able to manage to power so many LEDs from ordinary clock batteries, as each one usually takes a couple of volts and that would really mean a battery for each one. He was very clever in that respect — mind you, the batteries only lasted for about four minutes.

John put the suit on and, thankfully, it worked perfectly, as did the hat. He then had to put roller skates on to make his entrance. Everyone was terribly happy with the scene, and John was particular chuffed that all he needed to carry were a few small batteries. By all accounts he'd done something similar in the past and had ruddy great battery packs all over the place.

Another Bra

Working in television, at the BBC's White City studios, was quite a contrast from Bert's film work at Pinewood. It was also the first time he'd ever worked on a show that was filmed with a live audience, 200 people in this case.

That was pretty nerve-wracking, because I knew if anything went wrong during the recording, then I'd certainly know about it with 200 pairs of the public's eyes on me and the heckles. Previously it was just the crew that witnessed any of my cock-ups, rare as they were, thank goodness.

The shows were filmed, one a week, after a days rehearsal at the Shepherds Bush rehearsal rooms, and a full costume run-through on the floor before the recording. Planning was imperative as there was little time between rehearsal and recording for any ad lib gimmicks.

As previously mentioned, Bert had gained something of a reputation for snatching bras off. It was something he wanted to forget, but unfortunately, wasn't allowed to: The show's director asked if Bert could arrange a bra-snatch scene. With a groan, Bert explained:

This time round, it wasn't an actress but a counter top display dummy. A mannequin. I arranged the rig, as I had done on *Carry On Camping*, but then realized there might be a problem. You see, the mannequin was very lightweight and I was worried that the tension on my wire might cause it to topple over. I set everything up, and weighted the body a little too, then ensured the bra was held on with just one loose stitch. I pressed the button … it worked! Off flew the bra and up stood the mannequin.

As though destined never to work on a show that didn't involve bras of one form or another, Bert was again called upon by the director to make a very strange modification for the support garment.

It was the week before that show was due to be recorded, and so there wasn't that much time, and he explained to me this scene he had envisaged where the store was selling revolving bras. He wanted a counter top display with a bra that featured revolving boobs, and not only that, he wanted an actress to wear one of these things and show off her boobs (under her clothes I might add) going around.

I knew I only had a week, and was frantically thinking about what I might do. He then said that he'd also like a gent's pair of rotating underpants. Why not, I thought.

The bra was the worst thing to make. I used two electric motors and "cups" on the end of them, but I rigged it so that one motor turned clockwise and the other one went anti-clockwise — so the boobs rotated in different directions. That was really funny to watch. As well as the counter top display model, I had to think about the bra I needed for an actress to wear. Obviously, she didn't need to be a big-breasted lady, quite the opposite, in fact, as I wouldn't have had much room to play around with. The batteries, I thought, would sit in a handbag that she could hold, with the wires to the motor going up her arms and round.

The young lady who landed the part, Dominique was her name, came to see me for the fitting. She asked me if I was enjoying it, as she stood there naked from the waist up, and I said, no, I certainly was not — if it all worked at the end, I would, but until then, no, it was just work. Thank the Lord, it did work.

The revolving butt was another kettle of fish. I used the same technique of motors and cups, and took a large pair of y-fronts ... he put them on under his rather large-backed trousers.

The scene involved this couple walking into the store, and she was called over by Mrs. Slocombe [Mollie Sugden] to see the counter display. She then proudly said that she already had one, and opened her jacket to show off the revolving boobs. He then said, "I have the matching pants" and with that flipped up the back of his jacket and bent over, that was my cue and on came the motors. His two cheeks revolved in different directions, and dear old Mr. Humphries' eyes popped out of his sockets at the sight and he fainted. Oh, it really was so funny — at the end, that is. It wasn't much fun in the buildup as I was dreading it going wrong.

Pussy Cats

Bert was involved in several seasons of *Are You Being Served?* but admits there were only usually one or two gimmicks per show that involved him. He got on tremendously well with the cast and crew, and recalls most fondly his time with Arthur English, who played Harman, one of the "downstairs" general staff, and Mollie Sugden, who played the wild-haired, pussy-owning Mrs. Slocombe.

Again he, like me, was a Cockney and we hit it off immediately. He had a wonderful sense of humor. He remarried late in life, and he and his young wife had a child soon after. Sadly, he died when the child was very young and that was awful, so awful.

Mollie was terrific fun too. And, no, before you ask, I didn't get to see her pussy; that was the long-running joke in the series, Mrs. Slocombe's pussy cat. Her hairdos were something else on that show. One week it was purple, the next it was pink. Mollie really loved it though.

We went to rehearsals on Shepherd's Bush Green, and I always found myself, by some bizarre coincidence, getting into the lift with Mollie and her husband. We always arrived at the same time and had a chat in the lift; she loved a joke and a laugh. Upstairs we'd all have a cup of coffee and then launch into it. I was always on hand in case anything came out of the rehearsal that might work for that episode. Providing it wasn't anything too complicated or demanding, it would be done.

I didn't have a tremendous amount to do with Wendy Richard or Frank Thornton, who played Miss Brahms and Capt. Peacock, mainly because they were never part of any gimmick — that was usually Mollie or John. I remember Wendy as being a very quiet person, and never really had much to do with anyone off the floor. Nowadays I see her on *Eastenders* and she is, obviously, playing a very different character; but has done very well in my opinion to make that switch from comedy shows to drama. Not everyone can do it. Frank, again, was a very nice chap and I enjoy seeing him now on television's *Last of the Summer Wine*. He never seems to change.

Young Mr. Grace was played by the aged Harold Bennett, who was a rather elderly gentleman then, and he didn't really have to act — that was him. His character had a bit of a thing for the ladies, and he had this pacemaker-type device fitted so that every time he got excited — usually after catching a glimpse of leg — the buzzer and lights went off. So funny, and simple to make!

The show still repeats on television now, and I enjoy watching it very much as it stands up really well and is good, solid family entertainment.

The series has achieved something of a cult status in the U.S. and the actors are repeatedly asked over to make special appearances and attend fan club conventions. John Inman arrived at one such gathering a few years ago and was astounded to see queues extending around three blocks.

Spike

Following his work on *Are You Being Served?*, Bert was contracted for another of the BBC's comedy series, this time with Spike Milligan starring. Milligan had shot to fame as one of radio's *The Goons* along with Peter Sellers, Harry Secombe and Michael Bentine.

I was brought on board for part of the *Q7* series, and the entire run of *Q8*, and it proved to be a little hectic. I'd never met Spike Milligan before in my life, and was introduced to him at the rehearsal studios by the director.

The director then began explaining what they needed for one of the shows, but before he could finish, Spike took over. It was very much his series in every sense of the word you see.

"I want six dummies," he said.

"Right," said I. "I'll get you them."

"I want them dressed in Arab's clothes," he added.

"Well, that's down to wardrobe," I replied.

Anyway, off I went and got him six mannequins. I never really thought too much about it, to be honest, and just assumed the usual old clothes shop window type would do. I took them up to the center of London in a little van and took them to the wardrobe department, which was down a little one-way road somewhere near Hyde Park. There they were dressed in the Arab clothing Spike had asked for, before he arrived. Typical Spike, he reversed down the one-way street the wrong way in his mini. He said that he didn't want to drive all the way around the block to come in the right way, and maintained he wasn't breaking the law because he was reversing.

He looked at the mannequins and said, "Very nice, but I can't sling them, can I?" I was a little taken aback and asked what he meant. It turned out that the scene he had in mind involved him swinging these dummies around his head before throwing them down the street. He couldn't really do that with the ones I'd supplied. He wasn't angry or annoyed, as he realized he hadn't fully explained things to me, but said he wanted to do it again the next week and could I get him the sort of dummies he wanted.

Back to the drawing board, I thought.

I was, quite honestly, thoroughly disappointed when I returned home because it was the first time we had worked together, and as I didn't know him beforehand, I was afraid I hadn't made much of an impression. Well, not a good one.

A couple of hours of head-scratching followed in the Luxford household, before Bert hit upon an idea. He dashed out to his local men's outfitters and asked for six pairs of socks, six long-johns, six vests and a load of sewing material. He then returned home.

I sat down in my chair and started sewing. I'd decided to make six large rag dolls; they were fairly lightweight and, I thought, probably just the trick for what Spike wanted to do with them.

Then came the problem of what to stuff them with. Off I trotted to Uxbridge and bought ten large pillows. Casting puzzled looks at me, the store staff asked how many bedrooms I had.

"Two," I told them.

"Well, what are you going to do with all those?"

"I'm making some Arab dummies," I added, innocently.

I dread to think what they said about me behind my back, but their faces were a picture.

I made the dolls, stuffed them with the pillow filling and even painted on their faces. I was rather worried that Spike wouldn't like them, but again the following week, I loaded them in my van and drove to central London. I realized that it was pretty much make or break for me that day.

To my absolute delight, Spike came in and started dancing with excitement.

"Bloody great! Just what I wanted," he enthused.

I can't tell you what a relief that was to hear. From there on, I got to know Spike and his ways rather well and it worked out brilliantly between us.

Touché

Bert admits that Milligan's inventiveness and enthusiasm often generated some weird ideas, and they usually came thick and fast. Never before had Bert experienced that. A perfect example came on a location shoot, when the second assistant director approached Bert in his mobile workshop.

"I need a sword for Spike," he said.

Bert explained that he didn't have one — it wasn't mentioned in the script and nobody had told him that they might need one; it was, after all, a comedy show.

"Spike wants a sword," he said again, indignantly.

"Look," said Bert, "we're ten miles from anywhere, in the middle of nowhere."

"Can you perhaps make one?"

"Ah ... how long have I got?" inquired Bert.

To say he was shocked to be told 15 minutes is an understatement. Even back at Pinewood with his complete workshop, he'd be pushed to deliver. However, never one to say never, Bert said he'd give it a whirl.

Just outside the truck work-

Right: Spike Milligan vs. a snake, Q8. *Below:* Spike Milligan swallowed by the snake.

shop, Bert noticed a wooden fence consisting of hundreds of tall thin wooden stakes, linked by wire. One of the stakes was broken, and gave Bert the germ of an idea.

> I took the stake that was broken, and said to my assistant that we had knives and chisels so why not make something out of this thing. I cut it down to size, made a handle from the off cuts, carved it into a fairly reasonable shape, and sprayed it.
>
> Spike was amazed. I don't think he honestly thought we'd come up with anything.
>
> In my time with him, I had realized that very rarely did Spike want anything real. He liked things a bit larger than life, which helped bring out the comedy in situations. So the idea of a wooden sword supposedly being a real swashbuckling instrument really appealed. Apparently, I could do no wrong — although not by design, admittedly!
>
> I think it was then I fully appreciated Spike Milligan. He wasn't just a funny man, he was a clown genius who wanted to make people laugh above and beyond anything else.

Flying Cats

Further collaborations included "Funerals in Space," where a scaled-down coffin was attached to a model rocket and launched. Another rocket scene with Milligan and a cat inside an orbiting vessel called for the cat to float across the craft and out of a window.

> That one was done with fishing rods! Two, in fact. I had one to take the [toy] cat across part of the set, and my assistant took over with his across the rest and out the port hole. It looked so funny on screen. Hilarious in fact.

One of Milligan's take-offs was with the old BBC general knowledge show *Mastermind*, famed for its big black chair which contenders sat under a spotlight.

> Bob Todd, that wonderful comedy stooge, was to sit in the chair, and Spike wanted it to collapse as soon as Bob's backside touched it.
>
> I made a pretty good replica of the *Mastermind* chair, but a little bit more elaborate so the legs splayed outwards, adding to the comedy effect. I was conscious that Bob was advancing in years, and landing on the hard studio floor could have caused a nasty injury. I padded the chair rather substantially, and rigged the collapsible mechanism, which

was really just a cable release — as it was all held together by cables — electrically to a little box that I could hold several feet away.

A bit of comedy exchange followed, and as Spike asked the first question, he gave me the nod and the chair, along with Bob Todd, went crashing to the floor. I could never watch the real *Mastermind* after that without giggling.

Dear old Bob was great fun, and he was actually an old friend of mine too. One day they recorded a scene in which a lineup of men had their trousers pulled down. It was nothing to do with me, I must add. One by one the trousers were whipped off, and the chaps stood there in just their underpants. All except Bob, that is. Inadvertently they'd pulled his underpants down too and Bob didn't realize. Consequently he was standing there like a dummy, starkers from the waist down. Thankfully, he saw the funny side of it, and it was never broadcast. Although it's probably still lurking somewhere in the vaults at the BBC.

Oh, No, Another Bra!

Once again Bert's reputation for his work with brassieres had preceded him and, indeed, continued to haunt him. This time Bert was asked to make an inflatable bra for the *Q8* series. Not just any old inflatable bra, it must be added; on Milligan's instructions, it had to be a particularly big one.

Oh, yes, the inflatable bra. Again, it led me to Suitor's department store, and the ladies department. Remember, this was in the 1970s and men buying ladies underwear was not at all common.

Needless to say, I was greeted by a female assistant, and I told her, rather timidly, that I wanted to buy a bra.

"What cup size, sir?" she asked.

"I wasn't really thinking about a cup," I replied. "More of a pudding basin."

After a few scornful looks, she asked me who it was for. When I said a man, she did a double take and then started to treat me rather skeptically; but she saw that I was deadly serious.

A little while later, I left the store with a bra that could only be described as tremendous, in size anyway.

The next problem: how to inflate it effectively and with only the minimum of compact equipment (it all had to be concealed upon Milligan's person). A trip into neighboring Slough followed; Bert bought four rather large, strong balloons. Whilst in the shop, he asked the assistant if he had any ideas of how he might inflate them from, say, a back pocket.

He was very helpful, in fact, and suggested I pop into a bicycle shop down the road. They sold the loud horns that used to be around a lot, and they were powered by a carbon dioxide canister. One of those would easily tuck into a back or side pocket, and could be operated easily.

Off I went and got one.

I adapted the canister so that two pipes came out and wound their way up to the cups of the bra, where I'd attached the balloons. It was fitted on to Spike and I slipped the canister into his side pocket. It worked perfectly and was very funny indeed in the sketch.

Bulbs

Another rather unique Milligan request was for an inflatable doll, which he wanted to float across the top of the screen.

I went off to Slough again, to the same sex shop where I bought the enema bulbs. The chap behind the counter must have remembered me, or at least my strange request, as when I went in he said, "Oh, you're back — what is it this time?"

"An inflatable doll. It's not for me, it's for a film."

"What do you want it to do?" he asked.

I told him, and he suddenly produced one from under the counter that had a puncture in it, but he said it would be suitable for my purposes if I just taped it over and I could have it for less than half price. I do like a bargain. I never did ask how it got punctured. Perhaps I'm better not knowing.

I later inflated it with helium and off it went.

I don't know whether it actually made it to the transmission or not, as sometimes the director would have to censor some of the show when Spike got a little carried away in his ideas— quite a lot was cut on occasions. Mind you, Spike was very innocent in much of his comedy; it was more like schoolboy humor than anything else. I dare say, though, that a sex doll floating across the screen would lead to a few viewers picking up the phone, or putting pen to paper I should say as telephones were not that common in homes back then.

Milligan and Bert became good friends over the series, despite the onset haranguing and complaining from Spike (it was really just him showing off to the audience), particularly during rehearsals. Bert appreciates that it was all in good fun and he had a good-enough sense of humor to cope with it.

Scene Ten

Hillbillies, Flying Pigs, Splurge and Green Perspex

The hit American TV comedy show *The Beverly Hillbillies* ventured over the pond to London for an outing in Britain, and Bert got the call.

I knew of the show because it had been shown on TV here, and so when the company phoned through to say they needed me for a week, I was curious as to what effects they had in mind. From my recollection of the previous shows, there weren't any, really.

When I actually asked what would be required, the answer came back, "We don't know yet."

I said it would be helpful if they could give me some idea, as I might have needed to prepare certain things. Anyway, I had to content myself with the knowledge that there wouldn't be anything drastic.

They invited me over for breakfast at the Dorchester Hotel to meet the producer, director and stars. Very nice, I thought, and off I went.

The producer came over to me and looked quizzically at me before asking, "You're the special effects man, aren't you?"

"Yes, I am," I replied.

"Well, I have a little job for you."

I always cringe when I hear that, as there idea of little jobs and mine are usually totally different. As it turned out, it wasn't a big job at all.

"We have the Clampetts' truck over here with us, and I'd like you to look after it — be in charge of it," he said.

With respect, I pointed out to him that I'd never driven a truck in my life, nor a left hand drive.

"No, no, you don't have to drive it — it's just your responsibility. It's worth a fortune, so be careful and just make sure nothing happens. We have mechanics here, so don't worry about that side of it either."

It really wasn't an effects man's job, to be honest, more the transport department. I asked him if effects men in the U.S.A. would do this type of thing, and he said yes, all the time. I suppose there's quite a difference, or at least there was then, in the way we worked on each side of the Atlantic.

Bert guarded the truck with his life, and because he wasn't hands-on involved with any effects or filming, he was able to sit back to a certain extent and just enjoy it. Many amusing moments followed, particularly when the Clampett family (played by Buddy Ebsen, Irene Ryan, Donna Douglas and Max Baer, Jr.) drove around Eros' Statue in central London's Piccadilly Circus.

They were a great team to work with, so friendly and so warm; but it was a bit of a disgrace that I, as an effects man, didn't actually work on any effects. Don't tell anyone!

"Pigs in Space": Bert and the Pig space ship.

Muppets

Another popular American series on which Bert was drafted to work was *The Muppet Show.*

I'm not a Muppeteer, I must make that clear, and to be honest would probably make a bit of a mess of it if I tried. I was brought in to work on the "Pigs in Space" segment. They wanted a jet model of Miss Piggy — so I had to literally make pigs fly.

The rocket I made was about two and a half foot in

length, and made out of wood because it needed to be relatively lightweight and travel along wires, but still be rather sturdy.

It wasn't a particularly difficult commission, but very satisfying. I met Frank Oz on the show, and he was a Muppeteer who then went on to greater things in directing films. In fact, I had a lot to do with him on his big Pinewood film *Little Shop of Horrors*.

Feed Me!

Little Shop of Horrors was a musical adaptation of director Roger Corman's 1960 low-budget schlock horror. More precisely, it was a film version of the musical stageplay that was inspired by Corman's film. Along with snaring an Oscar nomination for Best Song, the Visual Effects team received a nomination.

There were something like a dozen Muppeteers on the film, principally involved with the "Audrey II" flesh-eating plant. The rest of the effects were really secondary to the plant, which was wonderful to see in action. You really would have thought it was real had it not been for the wires and cables coming out of the bottom. Having said that, though, on screen it looks very effective and very convincing. I certainly wouldn't want to get tangled up with it.

The sort of effects I was involved with were the ... well, what I call "incidental" such as the smashing of the clock when one of the arms of the plant came through a door. That was a fairly simple gimmick using a trolley and scaffold tube, which was "dressed" to look like an arm of the plant. I suppose it was more of an engineering exercise than anything else. I did other things such as breaking down doors and windows, in much the same way.

There were three of us on that one, involved in the non–muppet effects, and each of us had our own particular tasks—but we really were overshadowed by the marvelous Muppeteers. I could never have attempted what they achieved, I daresay I'd struggle with just an ordinary hand puppet; so in some respects, it wasn't exactly my scene, so to say, but the director made it a very enjoyable experience. Frank was, of course, a Muppeteer himself, as I've mentioned, and it was very apparent that he had a great enthusiasm for the Muppeteers on the film — more so than any other person or department. But you could hardly blame him for that.

Bugsy Malone. Pint-sized gangsters with splurge guns. (Gareth Owen Collection.)

Pint Sized Fun

In 1976, Alan Parker, a successful director of commercials, brought to life his first feature film, *Bugsy Malone*. It was an ambitious project in several respects: it was the director and producer's first feature film, it was a contemporary musical pastiche on the old American gangster era, and, er, the cast were all children. Financing was problematic, to say the least.

However, the film's executive producer David Puttnam eventually succeeded in twisting a few arms, and the story went before the cameras at Pinewood Studios. The pint-sized cast included Scott Baio and Jodie Foster, all touting guns. But not the traditional machine guns that people came to identify with gangster pictures, but rather ones that fired custard pies: splurge guns.

> I came onto Bugsy initially with the old smoke effects. Parker had all the sets built on rostra a few feet off the floor so as we could get underneath the "streets" and pump smoke through the manhole covers and drain outlets, etc. It all looked very convincing, too.
>
> Then, came the splurge guns. Hmmm.
>
> Malcolm King was the director of effects on the picture, and was at a loss at what to do. Just how do you fire splurge around a set? As I was considered a bit of an expert on guns, they came to me.
>
> Malcolm envisaged something like a tennis ball being fired that, when it hit a target, exploded with lots of cream coming out.
>
> I obviously realized that it would be very tricky, but the main problem would be in construction of the "ball" as when it hit someone, it would hurt. It was to be fired with compressed air, so it would also have to be strong enough to withstand the blow out, but not so tough as to need much force to burst on impact. The only thing I could think of was using a fine tissue-like "bubble" that would have to be made individually and be fired almost as soon as it was made. Otherwise the cream would soak through and the whole thing would just dissolve.
>
> We worked on it for a few days, and made the guns—that was the easy part. But in our testing, couldn't strike the right balance between

strength of the tissue and the force on impact to explode it. In fact, one volunteer was slightly concussed during testing.

A compromise was struck and the guns fired tennis balls for the desired effect but, on the cut, a prop man threw a custard pie at the child's face. That's the magic of filmmaking and editing.

Model car from *Bugsy Malone* presented to the director Alan Parker.

Over 1,000 custard pies were thrown in the film and 100 gallons of synthetic cream (the splurge) was used in all.

Of course, everything in the film was created in perspective to the young actors, including cars. There were about a half-dozen in all, fully functioning and pedal-powered, managing up to ten MPH. Each cost as much as a real Mini to manufacture, and was made by hand at Pinewood out of lightweight wood.

> One or two collisions and breakages occurred during rehearsals and back they'd come to the workshop for repairs. I was no stranger to them.
> Most of the cars went off to America after filming was completed, and I think Lord Montague got one for his motor museum. I also made a special model of the car for presentation to Alan Parker.

Ghostly Encounters

Television production continued to punctuate Bert's feature film work. For a one-off TV drama entitled *The Stone Tapes*, Bert was commissioned to make two specific pieces of equipment.

> The story went along the lines of how spirits and ghosts were living in the walls of this house, and some people who visited the house could see them whereas others couldn't. So a couple of experts were brought

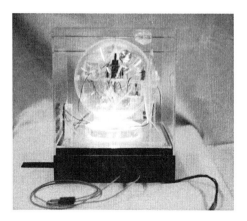 

The Stone Tapes, left: Sensor 1; ***right:*** Sensor 2.

in to set up some equipment to detect, once and for all, the presence of these spirits.

They brought in two instruments which did, in the end, detect them and subsequently exorcise them. These were what they wanted me for.

As usual, I didn't have any drawings or outlines, and it was left to me to get on with making the devices based absolutely on my imagination of what they might have looked like.

For the first device, I used a Perspex box which was about 18 × 18 × 18 inches, on a plinth, with a load of "mumbo jumbo" in it. It was totally useless, but it looked the part. The second was more of a pointer-detector device, again made up from odds and sods in my workshop. I know it sounds easy for me to say I made these things from bits of ... what you might really call *junk*, but they had to look technical and bits of wire and leftover electronic components were just the ticket for the job. Had I delivered a couple of boxes that looked like they'd had shoes in them, the producers would have gone potty and fired me, so the junk came in very handy and reassured me that all of the stuff I said "oh, I'll keep that, it might come in handy" about, did really come in handy. Remember that next time you're asked to tidy up the garage or loft!

The most difficult thing about this type of job is not having anything but a rough verbal idea of what is needed and a blank piece of paper. It isn't very easy to progress from there, believe me.

A Little Bang

No sooner had the ghosts been exorcised than a call came through from another TV show, the *Van Der Valk* production office none the less.

They needed a big car explosion in one of the episodes of the Amsterdam-set police series starring Barry Foster.

> It was only a little job, but they were prepared to fly me and Frank George over there to do it. Well, it sounded like fun and a couple of days away in Amsterdam — so off we went.
>
> Just for a giggle, I said to Frank that we "ought to do a 'before and after' photo." We did and as you'll see, we did quite a good job in blowing the car up.

Pinball Wizard

As the above stories illustrate, an effects man's role was rather broad at the time Bert was in the industry and could encompass everything from slamming doors, to designing and building gadgets, to snatching bras and blowing up cars. For his next feature, *Tommy*, Bert was asked to make an organ — a real church- or theater-type organ.

Top and bottom: Van Der Valk, before and after.

Left and right: Car/organ from *Tommy.*

It had to be quite a big thing, and we actually built it out of Fiberglas over the top of a Mini because it also had to be driven. That was ever so funny, as we had to make little peep holes for the driver to see out of as he drove this damn car around and around the studio. The organ didn't actually play, it was all dubbed in later. But you can't have everything.

We had a marvelous cast in that one, as there were lots of famous cameo players too. Ann-Margret, Oliver Reed, Roger Daltrey, Eric Clapton, Elton John, Tina Turner … the list goes on, and it was all directed by Ken Russell. Now, Ken had a bit of a reputation for doing rather strange things, and on this film it didn't wane, and this time it was baked beans. I kid you not when I say there was about half a ton of them on one set; the actors dived in and it really was a hell of a mess. Poor old Roger Daltrey was submerged in them. It made me shudder. Unfortunately I don't eat them very often, so I didn't draw many benefits from the set that time.

I was also involved with the Acid Queen, which Tina Turner brought to life, and all of the needles (about 100) and drugs that were pumped into this "lady" through pipes connected to the needles. They were all my doing and I filled the pipes with colored liquids that flowed all around, but appearing to go into her. It looked very attractive and a bit like a chemistry set.

Rekindling an Old Friendship

After their long and successful association on the Bond films, Bert teamed up with Sean Connery again in the 1980s on two feature films, *Outland* and *Highlander*.

Highlander called for large samurai swords to be made, as they were integral to the main action. Bert's services were engaged early in pre-production:

I was first asked to meet with Christopher Lambert at his apartment in London, as they wanted me to make breastplates for him. I expected a big, broad-shouldered, six-foot-tall bloke and couldn't have been more surprised to meet a chap my size. I explained why they wanted the breastplates made, for the battle scenes and for his own protection; they would be very light, but very strong. He was very nice about it all and I said all I wanted to do was measure him. Later we took a plaster cast of his torso and all of that went off to a foundry for the plates to be made.

I then had to make several replica swords in aluminum, as they had to be lightweight and safe for the actors. I made casts of the original swords and handles—which we then made in Fiberglas—from one original, which I still have.

The director, Russell Mulcahy, then told me that he wanted sparks to fly off the swords during the fight sequences. That was an interesting idea, I thought, and how kind of him to leave it at my desk.

I was stumped. I just didn't know what to do, to be honest. Then a chum of mine, Dave Ford, said "negative and positive, Bert." I was still none the wiser.

"Wire one sword up as the negative, the other as a positive and connect them across a 12-volt battery."

It seemed so simple, it was ingenious. So we had wires up Sean and Christopher Lambert's sleeves and trouser legs, around their what-cha-callits, or crown jewels if you like, and off them a battery. When the swords struck, they sparked. We then boosted the voltage to 24 volts and they sparked even better.

I think we worked for about two months solid on swords. Of course, being aluminum, they couldn't stand much force in the fight scenes and I was continually straightening and sharpening edges.

The main "Highlander" sword stood about four or five feet high to the hilt, and was very much like the old Crusader swords. That one I didn't keep, unfortunately. I know it sold at auction for a small fortune, and I still kick myself.

Working with Sean was very nice, but he wasn't actually on set for that long as he wasn't the main character. Of course, it was a totally different style of film to those we'd worked on before, but bloody good fun and it was good to see him again.

Bert had worked with Connery again a few years earlier to *Highlander* with a stint on *Outland*, again a very different genre of film, and it was rather aptly dubbed *High Noon in Space.*

Green Perspex

That was all made out of Pinewood, but set in space. One of the sets was a massive glass greenhouse construction, and I was asked to make a model replica. When I say model, I mean one on the scale of my living room — 12 × 10 feet — out of green Perspex. I still have a few sheets, and I'll tell you why …

Dave Ford and I made this great model and we used the Perspex that was sent to us by the art department. Each sheet was 6 × 10 foot and I think there were ten in all. After six weeks we stood back and admired our work. Then and only then did some bright spark realize that it was the wrong color Perspex. I couldn't believe it. We then had to take all of the damn stuff out and replace it with the new Perspex. I asked the art director if I could take a few sheets home to make ornaments for the cadets in my St. John's Ambulance troop; he was only too keen to get rid of it.

The finished model did look really nice, and the art department then made miniature plants and trees to go with it. I dread to think how much it cost in all, but I do know the original green Perspex cost over £1,000 alone.

Left: A fire-breathing dragon made by Bert for a television commercial. *Right:* The Hertz commercial eagle.

Bert Goes Commercial

Meanwhile, with commercial television growing in popularity, a greater number of adverts became more imaginative in their approach. It was another growing market which Bert had tapped into fairly early on.

The model for the Hertz eagle.

I can't remember how many adverts I worked on in total, as I only did a little work on some, whilst others were more demanding; but unlike features and TV series, I wasn't engaged for weeks at a time, it was more a day or two.

Some of the bigger things I had to do included making a large dragon, a flying saucer and, for a Hertz commercial, two large eagles which were to fly down and steal the windscreen wipers off a car. Now, I haven't been fortunate enough to see eagles close-up to study, but thought that they were similar in size to turkeys, and so bought a couple from my local butcher.

It was these large turkeys (which were dead, plucked and oven-ready) on which I based the body design and size — and it gave me something to physically get hold of and manipulate. The rest of the design I could garner from photographs.

Fortunately, the job came just before Christmas and so we had a rather large turkey dinner for free — mind you, we were the only family in the street to have a one-legged bird as I'd had to remove one of the legs to study the joints for my eagle. Waste not, want not.

Scene Eleven

Comedy, Fantasy and Sci-Fi

First there was *The Ten Commandments*, and then came *The Seven Deadly Sins*— not a Biblical epic like the former film, but a comedy treatment directed by long-time Peter Sellers collaborator Graham Stark.

I don't think it went down very well with the public, but it was a very funny film to work on. I had lots of lovely little jobs, most of which were spur of the moment ideas, but there was one specific sequence that was planned weeks in advance: I had to blow up a public convenience in a park.

The actor involved in the scene was Stephen Lewis, who was playing a park keeper who had it in for two particular chaps who used to come into the park everyday. They, in the story, collaborated to lure Stephen into this loo and blow him up in there. It was a prefabricated building built out of kilned plaster. I then had the plasterers department make three toilet basins for me, to go inside the three cubicles.

Graham said that he wanted the building blown up in one go. No problem I thought, I'll put in three 18-inch "bursters." Although they pack more of a visual effect with big balls of fire and smoke, they are still very dangerous and pack quite a kick when they go off. The idea was that the carefully placed devices would blow the walls out and the roof would then collapse. Graham was a bit like a schoolboy with his enthusiasm, and he started hopping up and down saying, "Make it good — make it big!"

Graham Stark

There was a back door to the building so Stephen could slip out without being seen, just ahead of my blowing it up. Graham gave me the signal once the cameras were rolling, in went Stephen and out of the back he came — then I pressed the button.

The structure literally shattered, the walls fell away, the roof fell down and there was a great big fireball. I couldn't believe what I saw next. The three toilet basins were still standing and out of the center one came this great pillar of smoke — one of my bursters had landed in there. I started apologizing but Graham was almost wetting himself in excitement. "I love it, I love it," he said.

I told him not to ask me to repeat it as I couldn't if I'd tried, but all was fine with the first take.

A Bit of a Temperature

One of the seven sins is gluttony, and that was my next assignment. Everything that this huge character in this sequence could eat, he ate. He was huge!

He was admitted into hospital, that was the story, and one of the nurses had to put an oral thermometer in his mouth, which he also ate. Graham told me that he wanted me to make a thermometer that he could film being chewed and swallowed.

I'd never come across anything like that before, so was at a bit of a loss as to what I could do. It had to be edible, safe and yet look convincing. I mentioned this to Linda, one of the young female cadets in my St. John's Ambulance troop whom I've mentioned before — she used to pop up to Pinewood to help me out occasionally. She thought the solution was obvious.

"Let's buy half a pound of clear glacier mints and melt them. You can make the mold and I'll melt them down."

That's exactly what we did. A full half-pound of mints went into a saucepan, with a quarter cup of water, and we boiled them until they melted. Meanwhile I'd made a mold by taking a real thermometer, from which I made a plaster impression, and lined it with silver paper. Linda poured the liquid in and we made six of the thermometers.

The next problem came with what we were going to use to color the bulb silver. It had to look like there was mercury in it. I trotted off to a local cake shop and bought a packet of little silver balls that are used to decorate cakes. We then melted them all down to a liquid and dipped our glacier thermometers in. They really did look like the genuine things and went down, quite literally, a treat.

For all of my experience, it took little Linda to come up with the idea. Perhaps I was thinking about complicated ways of doing it, whereas she saw a very simple way. I don't decry using other people's ideas at all, if they work, as that is what the business is about: adapting ideas and materials to create a certain effect. The simpler, the better!

Photos

Bert's association with Graham Stark continued after filming had wrapped, as both were very keen photographers and Stark often called by Bert's workshop.

He was fascinated with what we could do with effects in photography, and one day asked if I could loan him a smoke machine. He wanted to use it indoors for a photographic session. The one I gave him was adapted from a machine used mainly for diffusing insecticides in greenhouses, and therefore safe indoors, and I put some smoke oil inside. Five minutes later he was an expert on the machine and he later came up to show us some wonderful stills.

UFO

In 1970, Gerry Anderson's Century 21 productions made the sci-fi series *UFO* starring Ed Bishop at Pinewood and asked Bert to make them some futuristic computers.

Well, that was a bit of nonsense really — not the show, but what we made. We basically built these great big boxes with switches, rolls of magnetic tape spinning around and flashing lights. It was all cosmetic and they really didn't do anything but stand there, but then again that's what they wanted, so that's what we delivered.

 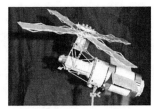 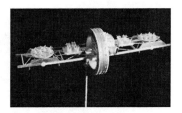

The Tomorrow People: Three space crafts.

Tomorrow

A few years later, another sci-fi series, *The Tomorrow People*, went into production. It was about a group of British teenagers with special powers: They were able to communicate with each other using telepathy. The series ran for almost 70 half-hour episodes.

They were exactly what the title said, people of tomorrow. They could go up into space under their own propulsion — they called it jaunting — and they had the most weird and wonderful space craft and weapons. I did have a lot of involvement in making the models of the ships, which were about three and a half foot long. As usual, I didn't have any sketches to start with but my idea of a spacecraft is a rocket shape with fins and I thought I'd do something around that idea. The producers didn't share my views, though, and wanted a spaceship with a gigantic center that revolved within itself.

When I asked them to elaborate on this somewhat vague description, they said that they envisaged two control mechanisms — skeletons on the outside — and the revolving part houses the people. Why did it revolve? To "keep" its own gravity. In truth, gravity doesn't stem from items revolving, but from the attraction of large mass such as the Earth; the smaller the planet, the less the gravitational force. So, in practice it was all a load of codswallop, but it would look good.

They explained that they wanted the Tomorrow People to fly through the air to the craft and enter. I then had visions of full-scale constructions being needed, but thankfully they heeded my advice and decided to do that part optically in post-production, thereby sticking with modest-sized models.

"How long have I got?" I asked.

"About six weeks," came the reply.

I went home and had many a sleepless night wondering how I'd make it all work and revolve. After a few stiff drinks, I launched into it. I placed an electric motor in the center, forming a core, and the outer parts [skeletons] were attached so as they would revolve, but without you seeing motors. That was the key to it all.

 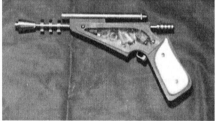

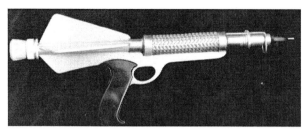

Three guns made by Bert for *The Tomorrow People.*

I was then asked to make the weapons for the characters to use, and again it was left to my imagination. I'm rather pleased with the finished items.

The Great Benny Hill

The Tomorrow People was filmed at Thames TV's Teddington Studios, where Bert was later engaged to work on their extremely popular *Benny Hill Show.*

Hill was unquestionably one of Britain's finest funnymen. Born in 1925, he was introduced by his grandfather to the world of burlesque, which he later drew on for his own routines. Born Alfred Hawthorn Hill, he took on the stage name of Benny Hill in homage to his favorite comedian, Jack Benny.

His first TV show aired in 1955 with a successful combination of impressions, songs and cheeky humor; it led to over 30 years of TV popularity.

His film appearances included *The Italian Job, Chitty Chitty Bang Bang* and *Those Magnificent Men in Their Flying Machines*–the latter two being productions Bert was involved with.

In 1979, *The Benny Hill Show* was shown in the U.S. and Hill became a massive star. His show are said to have aired in over 100 countries and brought much laughter to millions of people. Thames TV axed the show in 1989 for inexplicable reasons.

I did kind of know Benny after the film work, and went on to do quite a few of his TV shows; they were all very much for laughs and — like with Milligan — I had to supply all of the silly props and gimmicks for his sketches. Nothing of particular note, but important to the comedy. Like with Milligan, I was required to be around, just in case, and because I wasn't continually working, I could watch some of the fun unfold.

Contrary to his screen image, Benny was a very quiet and reserved character. He'd roll up at the studio with his carrier bag or briefcase full of scripts and ideas, then he'd go straight through to his dressing room and be on set soon after. He was quite close with Bob Todd and Jackie Wright (the little bald bloke) and their humor was very school boy-like, and very innocent; more slapstick than anything else. In the canteen, they'd be great fun to be around, but as soon as Benny went on set, it became a very serious matter: serious comedy.

Hill died a millionaire recluse in 1992, after completing a U.S. TV special. It was said that he never recovered from British TV dropping his show three years earlier.

Feeling the Heat

It was then back to the BBC for a series of *It Aint 'Alf Hot Mum*, a jungle-set comedy show with Melvyn Hayes, Windsor Davies and Michael Bates, made by the same team behind *Are You Being Served?*

I got on very well with the whole gang, but particularly Windsor Davies. We had several interests in common, and none were any good for us!

In one episode, which was actually the biggest thing we did in the series, we had to construct a "Bridge over the River Pong." It was left to me and one of the chippies at Pinewood to build this bridge, on location, across a river that was about 20 foot wide, and knee deep. We used one inch hem rope and slat which were about three foot wide and eight inches thick.

It took a good few days to make, and had to be strong enough to carry the main cast across. It did, thank goodness, bear their weight, but was very shaky — as these type of bridges are — and cause for a bit of unsteadiness as they all traipsed across. Poor little Don Estelle had to fall in, though, and I did feel for him as there wasn't much water in the river; it was more weeds, mud and rubbish! They were so concerned about the bridge that they didn't think about what was in the water.

It was supposed to be a really funny sequence, and was on screen, but for all of us involved on the set, it wasn't easy as we'd just learnt that Michael Bates, one of the leading actors in the series, had been diagnosed with terminal cancer. We all knew that underneath the happy exterior, Michael was very ill and in some considerable pain and that was very hard on all of us. He died soon afterwards.

Don Estelle and Windsor later released a record together, which they sang as their characters from the series, called *Whispering Grass*—which did rather well, if I'm not mistaken. [It reached number one on the British charts in June 1975.]

Having not been invited to perform the backing vocals on *Whispering Grass*, Bert decided to turn his attentions to another BBC TV favorite, *Dr. Who.*

Who?

It was the feature of *Dr. Who and the Daleks*, actually, and I was involved with the latter characters. They were not made at the BBC, but just down the road from Pinewood in Uxbridge at a firm called Shawcraft. I knew Bill Shawcraft very well, and it was he who made the first Daleks (with a young trainee named John Stears), and he also did all of the bits and pieces on the *Morecambe and Wise* shows for the BBC — everything from talking busts (the statue variety), to extra-long arms and legs for Eric to fool around with, to the smoke in the infamous Shirley Bassey episode where she sang "Smoke Gets in Your Eyes." Totally over the top, of course.

There were only ever four Daleks in the early years, but for this production they needed 20. Bill was then really retired, and he didn't have the premises any more, and so they approached us at Pinewood. I think we made 18 of them in the end.

I didn't have any drawing, but I did have pictures—what a luxury. They didn't have to move around much, which simplified things, but when it came to the "bubbles" on the outside of their bodies, we were a bit stuck as to what we should use.

Hang on, I thought, I'll go to Suitor's in Uxbridge to see what I could buy roughly four inches in diameter. I eventually ended up in the toy department, where they didn't really know me — they were about the only department in the store that didn't. I spotted these toy balls there which were about the right size.

Opposite, top: Cast from *It Ain't 'Alf Hot Mum*. **Bottom:** The bridge on the River Pong from *It Ain't 'Alf Hot Mum*.

"How many of these have you got?" I asked.

Now when you think about the Daleks, there are a lot of the "bubbles" on the body, and we had 18 to fit out. Quite a lot of balls.

"About 20, I suppose," the young lady said.

"Can you make it about 50?"

"Pardon?"

"Well, I need 50 as when I cut them in half it'll give me just enough," I explained.

She gave me a bit of a strange look and said she'd have a word with the manager and see what they had in the stores.

I eventually came out of the store with a giant bag that must have been big enough for me to get into, full of four-inch balls, and had to walk the length of the high street to my van. I won't repeat the comments I got.

Back at the studio I proudly displayed my purchase to my assistant, who was none the wiser. Now, the balls were plastic and it's not always easy to cut a ball in half, spot on, especially when they're not solid inside. The first thing we decided to do was drill a little hole in each one and fill them up with PVC foam. Each was filled separately and off to the lathe I went, spun them and cut a perfect circle with a sharp blade lined up exactly in the center. We rubbed them down, stuck them onto the hardboard bodies and sprayed them, before sticking on the sink plungers (they *were* sink plungers too) and lights which I bought from car spares shops.

Candid Camera

Award winning director Norman Jewison had previously lensed *Fiddler on the Roof* at Pinewood, and then returned with the ultra-violent futuristic *Rollerball*, starring James Caan and Ralph Richardson.

I only worked on certain sequences, not on the whole film. I guess it was more on the mechanical side of the production I was involved with.

The art director wanted a specific piece of equipment for one part of the film, and asked if I could come up with it — a remote-controlled video camera. Remember, this was in the mid–1970s and video cameras were really in their infancy, in terms of the domestic market, and I certainly didn't know much about them.

"I don't want it to necessarily work, but just look as though it's functioning — zooming in and out, moving side to side and so on," he said.

There wasn't anything on the market that did that, by remote control, so I didn't really have anything to refer to. However, I decided to go off to a big photographic dealership and talk to them about it.

The chap I spoke with behind the counter was intrigued. He said he could help me halfway by supplying me with a little video camera that had an automatic zoom. It was quite expensive, but I needed it!

The first thing I did was take it back to my workshop and take it to pieces. As soon as I figured out how it worked, I put it back together. Then I bought two tiny electric motors, another (fake) lens and put them together so the motors (turning alternately) controlled the zoom — which was basically achieved by revolving the lens. Underneath, I attached another motor which turned the camera around on a swivel. Of course, I was able to control the motors remotely, and so by virtue of that, it was a remote-controlled camera. It didn't actually work in terms of it recording onto tape, because I didn't need it to, but could have done quite easily with a real lens and few more modifications. Had I done that, it would have probably been the first fully functioning remote-controlled camera. I could have made my fortune. Ah, well...

Man of Steel

The first three episodes in the *Superman* film franchise were lensed at Pinewood, along with part of the fourth, *The Quest for Peace*. But in typical Alexander Salkind tradition, they never shot one film at a time. Most of *Superman II* was in the can before they'd finished the first movie. When Bert was drafted in to assist with certain effects, he wasn't sure which episode he was working on.

I was very much a background man, as Colin Chilvers was the director of effects on the pictures. Principally, I was involved in the pyrotechnics and all of those wonderful big explosions when the sets were destroyed. Colin wasn't a hands-on man in the sense that he would physically roll up his sleeves and work on the stage floor, but he was very good coming up with the ideas and methods and did an admirable job directing the effects which people like me worked on. There were many different sorts of effects on the films, of course, because there were extensive flying sequences, miniature and matte work with people like Roy

Kryptonite prototype from *Superman*. (Robin Harbour.)

Field and Derek Meddings (who won Oscars for their work) and Cliff Culley. On some of the bigger stage sets, there were up to another five or six of us working on the physical effects.

For *Superman II*, I was asked to orchestrate a scene in a car breakers yard where Superman, as played by dear Christopher Reeve, who is now tragically paralyzed, was standing and old tires were thrown one after the other over him, with him eventually being the core in an eight-foot high column!

That was done, similar to Oddjob's hat in *Goldfinger*, using wires, but we couldn't use real tires because of their weight — we'd have needed big thick cables which would have been easily visible on screen — and the actors couldn't have slung them. The tires I made were painted polystyrene, and the camera speed was slowed down a little so as when the film was later run at normal speed, the tires appeared to be flying at a fair old whack.

On *Superman III* I had a lot to do with Richard Pryor and the great big computer room hideaway, with Robert Vaughn calling the shots in a bid to control the world's weather. The script called for the lair to be destroyed at the end of the film, and so Colin Chilvers walked me through the set saying, "I want a bomb there … a lot of sparks there … smoke coming up from here" and so on. The space was fairly confined, and with all of these fireworks going off— and they were literally fireworks like those you see on Guy Fawkes night — we had to take extra-careful precautions as you're never quite sure where these things end up, and with a big crew and cast on the stage, you can't afford to make a mistake. So it wasn't just a case of shoving things here and there, I had to work it all out, almost mathematically. The director [Richard Lester] wanted a good five minutes of film, and fireworks don't last that long unless you have a few hundred. That's a lot of heat, smoke and fire to control.

In that sort of situation, you have to make sure, when rigging the set, that not one falling spark or firework will accidentally trigger another firework, because then it all runs away with itself. That's the difficult part! I think it took five or six days to film in the end after a week of my planting the charges, shooting each little part separately. Colin supervised it extremely well and had a brilliant planning mind for large-scale effects consisting of many little effects all joined together.

Hawk

A curious little sword and sorcery picture called *Hawk the Slayer* made its base at Pinewood. Starring Jack Palance, John Terry and Bernard Bresslaw, the story concerned two brothers—one good, the other evil—competing for possession of a magical sword.

Oh, no, not another sword film, I thought! It was quite a modest-budget picture, with lots of local locations such as Black Park, over the back fence of Pinewood's perimeter.

The director said that he wanted a sword with, at the pommel, a hand clasping a "green egg." It was supposed to be the Elfin Minestone which had magical powers. Oh, yes, I thought, here we go.

We made the original sword ourselves, and the plasters department made a lightweight Fiberglas one. He told me that the sword (minus the "egg") was to come up from wherever, with the hand open, and he wanted the egg to travel across the room and into the hand, which then closed over it, holding the egg in place.

We got the old fishing rods out again for that sequence! There were two of us, in fact, each with a rod; my colleague Bill Cohen handled the initial elevation of the egg and part-travel across the set and I took over for the rest and the bit where the egg landed in the hand and started glowing. That was done with an optical effect, whereby the color, or glow, was added in later.

The egg had magical powers such that whenever the owner of the sword (in this case, Hawk) thought about it, it flew into his hand. And that was what Hawk's evil brother [Palance] was after.

The second thing the director, Terry Marcel, said he needed was a load of colored smoke, which was to cover half of Black Park ... or so he thought.

I asked him what sort of budget he had allocated for this, and whilst he didn't mention a specific figure, he maintained that it would be enough. I asked him if he knew how much a smoke canister cost. He didn't. I said that they were £20 each (and this was 20 years ago, you must remember) and on top of that, I said, there was no such thing as colored smoke, only black or white. Colored smoke is actually made by mixing a very delicate colored powder with the smoke canister, and that powder is then dispersed like soot all over the area. So he'd be covering Black Park with all the colors under the rainbow—and that would need to be cleared up.

"Mmmm," he said, "I don't think I'll have any colored smoke. Black and white will be fine."

My assistant and I then spent about two weeks running around Black Park with smoke guns. We didn't see much daylight through it all.

There were lots of peasant cottage and forest fires, and that sort of thing, which we also worked on. It was a fun film to do, but as Jack Palance said to me, it wasn't exactly Oscar material—he was rather more fruity in his language. I think it was one of those sort of projects that sounded like a good idea on paper, shall we say.

Christmas Is Coming

Following his work on Alexander Salkind's *Superman* films, Bert was invited to join his big-budget production of *Santa Claus — The Movie* which was, like *Superman*, a total fantasy picture.

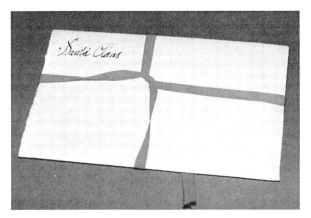

A letter to Santa Claus from *Santa Claus, the Movie.*

That really was a lovely film to work on. It was such a great team, both in front and behind the camera, and a lovely storyline — everybody loves Santa.

I had a lot to do with the toys and gimmicks in Santa's factory, and everything was real on that set — nothing was fake. I'd estimate, conservatively, that it cost about half a million pounds. There were lots of lovely little gimmicks and toys in the factory, and lots of conveyor belts carrying them, like the wooden men with drums which were all made in the studio workshops, and the little sticks of rock and toys in the back of the sleigh. Really charming things, and visually very pleasing.

Speaking of Santa's sleigh, it produced some controversy, to be honest, with the reindeer. You see, we had real animals for certain scenes, and then there were mechanical ones, made by a special dedicated "animatronics" unit. The controversy arose when it became known that they'd used real reindeer skins on the mechanical models.

We had a few problems with the sleigh in trying to achieve the 180–degree rotation and in some of the launching sequences (the flying was all done using miniatures). The damn thing was so heavy it never did what we wanted.

I supervised other scenes involving snow and weather effects, which I'll discuss in general in the next chapter — that's interesting work in itself!

Aliens

Bert's last feature film, before he retired, was another biggie —*Aliens*, with Sigourney Weaver. Just like on his first feature, his work on his this was principally engineering-based.

> I suppose I was on the production for around two months, and was involved primarily with the spaceship mechanics; the moving seats on rails, for instance. They cost an absolute bomb to make, as the invoice I got through for the rollers and tracks alone was over £2,000. It was a rather large-budget film so thankfully that didn't seem to bother them. It amazes me sometimes to think that on some productions I got sour looks if a major effect cost a few hundred pounds or more, and yet an incidental thing like on *Aliens* costing thousands didn't get a second glance. What a funny business we're in.
>
> Most of the film's effects were handled and supervised by John Richardson, who did a marvelous job. He's still in great demand nowadays I'm pleased to say. He grew up in the business as his father Cliff was a great name in effects and a tremendous friend of mine. It's very satisfying to see someone like John rise through the ranks and do so well, but to then see him win an Oscar for his work — as he did with *Aliens*— is brilliant, absolutely brilliant.

SCENE TWELVE

The Elements

For effects men, the weather is an important factor, and specific elements are required to perform in specific film and TV scenes.

Many people have this false illusion of someone standing on the corner of a set with a hose pipe squirting water into the air to create rain. There's a bit more to it! Rain is controlled by what we call rain bars, which are horizontal pipes suspended quite high above the set. Obviously, as well as creating the rain one has to be concerned with where it goes, so on stages, for example, everything had to be lined with polythene and the water channeled off the stage.

In my day, the flow of the water into the bars which created the rain effect couldn't be controlled by the likes of me; the unions dictated that anything to do with water had to involve plumbers. So every time I wanted a rain shower, I had to hire in a plumber to turn the taps on and off, up and down, as I instructed. It was bloody idiotic, but the only way we were allowed to do it. The more you turned the tap on, obviously, the greater the pressure and the greater the downpour. I'd tell them where I wanted the rain bars, whether they were to be separately controlled or not, and then it was just a case of deciding on the pressure — shower, or cats and dogs!

Water effects were very much in evidence during the filming of *The World Is Not Enough*, James Bond's nineteenth official filmic adventure. One visitor to the large outdoor Pinewood tank, over which was constructed a large Caspian Sea caviar factory, was agog to see the little waves and ripples in the water being generated by two skin divers bouncing empty barrels up and down. In these days of advanced technology, surely they have machines to do that?

Yes, they do. But, as I keep saying, as my mentor told me, "If you can pull it with a piece of string, then use a piece of string."

Wave machines are in existence, and used in a great many swimming pools, and are based exactly on the bouncing barrel idea. These machines were invented by Jimmy Holt, who was based down in Southall and later owned the water tank out in Malta, and are about 20 foot across and have several barrels on hydraulic rams — as one goes up, another goes down and waves are created. Jimmy could create waves up to 20 foot high with his machines, but for smaller waves and ripples you wouldn't really look to the machines.

You've also got the "buckets" which are like slides in children's playgrounds but with a 60-gallon water tank at the top. They take a fair amount of time to fill up, but when they've tipped, they create a sudden and powerful force of water. The beauty of the buckets is that you can move them around a set and create the desired effect, whereas with the wave machines you have to have a tank of water.

When it came to snow, it didn't involve water (or the freezing of it) and so the effects man was allowed to work it himself.

The most common, or popular if you like, way of creating snow is to sieve it from high above using a very long container, about six foot long, which is vibrated. Polystyrene is used, but not just any old sort as regulations are quite specific: it has to be fireproof because it's falling around very hot lamps and other electrical equipment, and a thick covering on a stage floor could easily be ignited by a stray spark from somewhere and take the whole stage up.

Snow is easy, but fog on the other hand is a pain in the backside. There are two ways of making a fog: dry ice or smoke oil.

I much prefer dry ice as it's very safe and harmless. You can switch the machine on and off and control the flow very easily and quickly. However, it's very expensive because each block of dry ice is upwards of £10. You can easily use 50 blocks in one afternoon, so it's by no means economical.

The smoke oil technique originated in America and was based on the insecticide machines used in large greenhouses and the like. Of course, they used DDT and other chemicals in these which are very dangerous if inhaled, but we — in adapting them — used a standard harmless smoke oil. You'd see them used on old–London set films, such as *Sherlock Holmes* and some of the Hammer horror films.

Perhaps the oddest weather effect, in terms of film, is wind because it is undoubtedly the noisiest (and a sound recordist's worst nightmare).

You can't create wind without noise (or smell in some cases!). There are two types of wind machines—electrically propelled and petrol—both are really giant fans.

The electric ones are undoubtedly the quietest, but then you've got all of the cables that go with them, and if you're out on location, it's not always easy. With the petrol motor-propelled ones, there is an immense amount of noise, they're mainly Volkswagen engines, but there were a couple of Spitfire ones too which fascinated me given my RAF background; they were the Merlin Mk VIIs. I believe that there were a few Hurricane engines in use too—usually with about 1,000 RPM; much more and they'd take off. Of course, you know how much noise they generate and so they had to be a long way away from the actors, but with strong wind and hurricane effects, you had to be a lot closer. That meant the dialogue often had to be dubbed later on.

In combining rain and wind, you could stir up a great storm. In films set at sea, for instance, with tremendous gales and storms, we'd often just direct a fire hose into one of the wind machines. Simple.

The other element of course, is fire. *The Firechasers* was probably one of the biggest fires ever arranged in a British production, but there are many types of fire, including very small ones—and they're sometimes just as tricky to arrange and control.

In *Carry On Camping*, Terry Scott bent over a bit too close to his camping stove and his bum caught fire. Now, although you're only dealing with a relatively small flame, it's on an actor, and that's potentially dangerous. You might laugh when I tell you this, but we fitted Terry with a pair of asbestos underpants, a pad at the back and then we just covered his shorts with a bit of rubber solution and he did the rest by bending over near the flame. It sounds easy, I know, but you have to know exactly what you're doing and how much rubber solution to use, the thickness of the asbestos and how long it needs to be alight—and, of course, you have to have a fire officer on standby with an extinguisher.

The safety of artists and crew was always of paramount importance to me. When an actor was going to be near a flame, for example, as a precaution I always coated his or her hair with a special fireproof gel, as hair is very flammable. Similarly, we could apply gel to hands and faces, as required.

I've never, thankfully, had a case of accidental burning in my career, but there was one incident where a foolish actor wouldn't take my advice and got very hot, shall we say, as a result. He was sprinkling magic dust (which was actually a little bit of gunpowder compound, like you'd have in a firework) into a fire in this one particular scene, which was supposed to fuel the fire momentarily (like throwing a bit of petrol on it). I told the actor in question to stand to the side of the fire and throw the dust into it, rather than sprinkle it over the top of the flame. He wouldn't listen and the director said he could do what he wanted, so I told him that it would be on his own head and walked away. Believe me, when he sprinkled the dust over the flame, he moved away bloody quickly, shaking his hand.

Never compromise safety for the sake of an effect — it's only a film, after all.

SCENE THIRTEEN

Effects Nowadays, and Simplicity Is Still the Best

I know I've already commented on effects nowadays and how some-times computers are used simply because that is how the modern-day effects crews have been brought up.

For instance, when *Jurassic Park* hit the screens in 1993, people said that it changed the effects business as we know it. True, to a certain extent, it did. Nobody can say they've sat through the film and not been impressed or over-awed with the sheer spectacle of it all, I mean, those dinosaurs looked pretty damn real to me. Naturally, when one com-pares that to the work of Ray Harryhausen on say *Clash of the Titans* or *Jason and the Argonauts*, then Ray's work may be mistaken as looking very "amateur." But you must remember the technology available at the time of making those latter films was pretty primitive, and Ray did a wonderful job. You show me any kid who seen his monsters and wasn't just a tiny bit scared. However, what you must remember is that if Ray hadn't been around and hadn't developed the stop-motion technology, then *Jurassic Park*—as we know it—might still be a few years away. It's a bit like the illusions I mentioned earlier; more often than not, mod-ern-day illusions are based on old ones, but jazzed up a bit.

There are times, of course, where computer technology is vital to the success of a scene. For instance, on the last Bond film *The World Is Not*

Enough, the "caviar factory" set attack used helicopters with buzz blades. That was filmed on a set with actors running around, and would have given the insurance people (not to mention the actors) a nightmare! So computer-generated blades were "inserted" after shooting. When one of the helicopters crashed and the circular blades flew across the set, "chasing" Robbie Coltrane — that was all CGI (Computer Generated Imagery) too. But in using that technique, you have to plan very accurately as the actors are effectively acting with nothing, and Robbie was running from ... fresh air. But his expressions, timing, route and the like have to be planned with military preciseness if the computer stuff is going to fit properly. So the old adage of "oh, we'll fix it with CGI" doesn't work for me, as it's got to be planned!

Looking at another recent blockbuster, *Gladiator*, there are some marvelous computer effects, in particular, the establishing shot of Rome and the Coliseum. Fantastic. But expensive! If the camera moves across a scene, as it did with this shot I mentioned, then that immediately doubles (or even more) the cost of the CGI shot, as then you have a moving subject and surroundings.

In the "old days" we'd have used matte painting techniques, and whereas you might argue they never stand up to the digital technology nowadays, I would argue conversely.

Let me tell you a little story.

There can't be many people who haven't seen *Star Wars*. When it was first released in 1977, it was the most talked-about picture in the business. The effects were brilliant.

After *The Spy Who Loved Me* was released in 1977 (and lost out in the Oscar stakes to *Star Wars*!), Cubby decided that the next Bond film should be *Moonraker*, to cash in on the current space interest, as NASA were preparing to launch their first shuttle.

There were lots of sequences involving space shuttles, the space station, actors, fight sequences and the like. My old mate Derek Meddings was in charge of effects on the picture and the thought of having to achieve all of these sequences was quite something. There weren't the computer effects that we have today, and there wasn't an infinite budget or time scale either.

Derek decided to use miniatures for everything, and an old camera wind-back technique.

Whilst the main units transferred to studios in Paris, Derek stayed behind at Pinewood with his model unit. There he constructed scale modes of the shuttles and space station.

He lined the walls of the 007 stage with masses of black velvet, and in the velvet used little bulbs to represent stars.

The trick of camera wind-back sounds simple, but it's quite an art form. In essence, you shoot one sequence, rewind the film and shoot another over it, rewind the film …. and so on. What this enabled Derek to do was film one of the shuttle docking on the station, wind it back to shoot another shuttle docking, etc., and he maintained perfect focus on all of the shuttles in the completed sequence (which you'd never get if shooting all at once). To expose only the correct section of film, a large black matte box is used on the front of the lens. You can then (using a matrix) decide which sections you're going to expose. So you might open up square A1 for one pass, then A2 for another, then maybe B2, etc., etc. This could go on for as many as 30 or 40 wind-backs of the film, so you can imagine that one slip towards the end can bugger up weeks of work!

Another thing Derek had to think about was the stars. He shot the space station on its own initially, with stars twinkling, but realized that on wind-back to shoot the shuttles, the stars would be on film already, meaning they would show through the shuttle as it passed over them.

Being an intelligent sort, Derek mapped out the course of the shuttles and using little variable resistors, effectively turned down the stars (bulbs) as the shuttles passed over.

When you see this sequence on *Moonraker* next time, take a good look. That was all achieved in-camera. It's pretty impressive and shows what can be done. The sequences cost a fraction of what the Star Wars did too.

Whilst I don't dispel computer technology as being important, I would just say that sometimes the tried and tested ways can provide an equally good result, and that shouldn't be lost sight of.

SCENE FOURTEEN

Breaking In

Coming into the special effects industry nowadays is perhaps a little easier than when Bert started out, given the greater use of, and need for, effects in films— opportunities are greater. However, as Bert (now dubbed the grandfather of effects) is quick to point out, one cannot just expect to walk in to a studio and become an effects engineer:

You have to have a background in what I would call a science-based subject: physics, chemistry, electronics, maths, engineering and so forth. In my day, you came in with a trade, in my case engineering, and developed in that particular area and, in a roundabout way, moved into the other areas little by little, training on the job. There was no actual training course for effects *per se*. As a youngster, I was fascinated by chemistry and had my own little laboratory in the house — I nearly blew myself up a couple of times in making hydrogen! So the seeds were sown early with me.

Later on, as I've already mentioned, it was really by Syd Cain coming into my workshop with his idea for the attaché case in *From Russia with Love*, that I moved into effects from engineering. Others of my colleagues had family connections in the trade, or were just dragged in to fill a gap — that's how *we* developed in the business.

But once you start on the ladder, it is a long climb before you can say you're fully qualified and adept in, say, using pyrotechnics. You can expect to train for five years before you're granted a license! Similarly with firearms.

Now, of course, the BBC run courses and film schools offer an introduction into the trade, but really you do need the practical experience,

185

Bert, Joe Fitt, Paul Weston (stunts), Dave Worrall (author), George Leech (stunts), Peter Lamont and the Aston Martin DB5. (Graham Rye.)

and that scientific background which will enable you to move on and make your own way.

So if anyone tells me that they're interested in breaking into the effects business, I tell them to get a good grounding at college first and prepare for a long hard slog — it'll be a good few years before you're blowing things up on your own. Ultimately, though, it's about being careful *and* entertaining, and if you can achieve both of those, you'll be around for a long time and I should know.

Retirement

As for me, I'm now enjoying my retirement and spending time with the family — the ever-increasing family! I'm not only a grandfather, but great-grandfather too. So far none of the clan have shown any great desire to work in the film industry — sensible lot. But you never know.

Keeping a hand in, though, and rather enjoyably, I'm often invited to gatherings of the James Bond Fan Club when they have functions at Pinewood. They're usually very enjoyable days with a good crowd. Without wanting to appear immodest, I do get asked to sign books, photographs and autographs from the assembled, and at one such do I sat down for an entire afternoon doing just that — with the publication and launch party for the Aston Martin DB5 book *The Most Famous Car in the World*. My wrist ached for quite a while after that. It's all good fun, though, and quite bizarre to think about really: from a once-young engineer in Chiswick to autograph signings at the world-famous film studios.

The main thing is though, it *was* great fun and I was very lucky. I hope you've enjoyed sharing in my ramblings — and maybe even learnt a thing or two?

Afterword

by John Richardson

I remember meeting Bert back in the '60s, I was working with my father Cliff, and Bert was in the Pinewood Studios Effects Department with Frank George and Jimmy Ackland-Snow. The first pocket calculator had

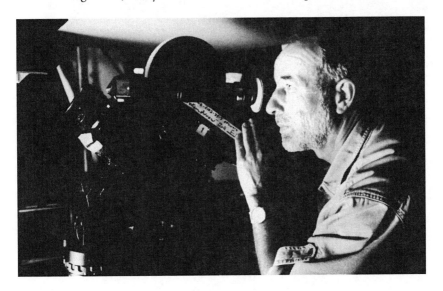

John Richardson

not been made then and home computing was unheard of. When one made an effects gadget or built an effects rig, it *had* to work on set. We did not have the luxury of being able to "fix it in post" or remove the wires afterwards. Unfortunately, with onset of the digital age many of the classic arts of filmmaking have been lost. The ability to get the shot "in camera," often using time-proven techniques, is a skill that is disappearing rapidly. The advantage of many of those gags was the look of reality that they gave. They were also very cost-effective and everyone could see the result at dailies the next day.

Bert was from this era. A boffin, he was always at home in the workshop and I can recall many instances where his calm logic was just what the crisis needed. There were numerous occasions when I would go into the shop and get him to make something for me. The wonderful thing was that he always understood what I wanted before I had finished telling him what it was. He knew that we would need it "last week" and I knew that he would have it ready. The variety of the work and the films over those years was vast, from *The Battle of Britain* through *The Devils* and *Rollerball* to James Bond and *Aliens*. Bert was always there, solid as a rock, a true professional. By the way, did I mention his sense of humor?

March 2000

Filmography

The following are the films for which Albert J. Luxford did special effects work, in chronological order. Dates are the first U.K. release dates and do not necessarily correspond to the actual production date, or to the order on which Bert worked on them.

P–producer, D–director, AP–Associate Producer, W–writer, DOP–director of photography, M–composer, PD–production designer

Dr. No

1962. Color.
P: Harry Saltzman & Albert R. Broccoli, D: Terence Young, W: Richard Maibaum, Johanna Harwood, Berkley Mather, DOP: Ted Moore, M: Monty Norman, PD: Ken Adam

CAST: Sean Connery, Joseph Wiseman, Ursula Andress, Anthony Dawson, Bernard Lee, Eunice Gayson, Lois Maxwell.

The first of the James Bond films based on Ian Fleming's novels. The titular metal-handed villain embarks upon a missile-toppling plot from his Jamaican hideaway. Fast-moving, fast-paced and intriguing story with exotic locations, sexy women, violence and tongue-in-cheek humor which became the series' secret to box office success.

The Iron Maiden

1962. Color.

P: Peter Rogers, D: Gerald Thomas, W: Vivian Cox, Leslie Bricusse, DOP: Alan Hume, M: Eric Rogers

CAST: Michael Craig, Alan Hale, Jr., Jeff Donnell, Cecil Parker, Noel Purcell, Roland Culver.

A steam traction engine race is featured in this film, which attempts to emulate the success of the vintage car race movie *Genevieve*, but with less success.

Call Me Bwana

1962. Color.

P: Harry Saltzman, Albert R. Broccoli, D: Gordon Douglas, W: Nate Monaster, Johanna Harwood, DOP: Ted Moore, M: Monty Norman, Muir Matheson, PD: Syd Cain

CAST: Bob Hope, Anita Ekberg, Lionel Jeffries, Edie Adams.

Bob Hope has built himself a phony reputation as an intrepid explorer of the African jungles. When his services are called upon to rescue a recently returned (and lost) American space probe in the jungles, many comic adventures result.

Dr. Syn Alias the Scarecrow

1962. Color.

P: Walt Disney, AP: Bill Anderson, D: James Neilson, W: Robert Westerby, DOP: Paul Beeson, M: Gerard Schurmann

CAST: Patrick McGoohan, George Cole, Tony Britton, Geoffrey Keen, Kay Walsh.

Based on Russell Thorndike's novel, the story follows the Vicar of Dymchurch's alter ego, the Scarecrow, who is a smuggler and often outwits the authorities. The character is portrayed more as a hero than villain. This story was initially filmed 25 years earlier by Michael Balcon (latterly of Ealing fame).

A Stitch in Time

1962. B&W.

P: Hugh Stewart, D: Bob Asher, W: Jack Davies, DOP: Jack Asher, M: Phillip Green

CAST: Norman Wisdom, Edward Chapman, Jerry Desmonde, Jeanette Sterke.

In this incarnation, Norman Pitkin is a hapless butcher's assistant who — when the shop is held by an armed robber — urges his employer Mr. Grimsdale to swallow a valuable pocket watch rather than have it stolen. A hospital spell follows with many slapstick routines, and a love interest coming onto the scene.

From Russia with Love

1963. Color.
P: Harry Saltzman & Albert R. Broccoli, D: Terence Young, W: Richard Maibaum, Johanna Harwood, DOP: Ted Moore, M: John Barry, PD: Syd Cain
    CAST: Sean Connery, Lotte Lenya, Robert Shaw, Daniela Bianchi, Pedro Armendariz, Bernard Lee, Lois Maxwell, Eunice Gayson, Desmond Llewelyn.
    James Bond is lured into helping a Russian cipher clerk defect to the west, the prize being a sought-after Lektor decoding machine. But evil doings are afoot as SPECTRE plans to pit East against West and Bond is the tool.

The Horse Without a Head

1963. Color.
P: Walt Disney, D: Don Chaffey, AP: Hugh Attwooll, W: T. E. B. Clarke, DOP: Paul Beeson, M: Eric Rogers
    CAST: Leo McKern, Jean-Pierre Aumont, Herbert Lom, Pamela Franklin, Vincent Winter
    Enthralling children's adventure from the Disney stable following a group of crooks and their endeavors to recover stolen money hidden in a toy horse.

Billy Liar

1963. B&W
P: Joe Janni, D: John Schlesinger, W: Keith Waterhouse, Willis Hall, DOP: Denys Coop, M: Richard Rodney Bennett
    CAST: Tom Courtenay, Julie Christie, Wilfred Pickles, Mona Washbourne, Rodney Bewes, Leonard Rossiter
    An undertaker's clerk in a dreary northern town lives in a world of fantasy and many interesting scenarios ensue as he "escapes" his humdrum life. A TV series and stageplay adaptation followed.

Doctor in Distress

1963. Color.
P: Betty E Box, D: Ralph Thomas, W: Nicholas Phipps, Ronald Scott Thorn, DOP: Ernest Steward, M: Norrie Paramour
    CAST: Dirk Bogarde, James Robertson Justice, Samantha Eggar, Donald Huston, Dennis Price.
    The fourth of the *Doctor* films marked Bogarde's return to the series, albeit only for one last outing. In this episode Simon Sparrow goes to work for Sir Lancelot Spratt, who is taken ill and falls in love!

Carry on Spying

1964. B&W

P: Peter Rogers, D: Gerald Thomas, W: Talbot Rothwell, Sid Colin, DOP: Alan Hume, M: Eric Rogers, PD: Alex Vetchinsky

CAST: Kenneth Williams, Charles Hawtrey, Barbara Windsor, Bernard Cribbins, Eric Barker, Jim Dale.

Dr. Crow, evil genius behind STENCH (The Society for Total Extinction of Non Conforming Humans) has stolen the secret — Formula X and it is left to the new recruits of BOSH (British Operational Security Headquarters) to retrieve it.

Goldfinger

1964. Color.

P: Harry Saltzman & Albert R. Broccoli, D: Guy Hamilton, W: Richard Maibaum, Paul Dehn DOP: Ted Moore, M: John Barry, PD: Ken Adam

CAST: Sean Connery, Gert Frobe, Honor Blackman, Harold Sakata, Shirley Eaton, Bernard Lee, Desmond Llewelyn, Lois Maxwell.

Auric Goldfinger's fascination with gold leads him to Fort Knox — the world's largest depository. He doesn't intend to rob it, merely explode a small nuclear device inside the vault, rendering it all radioactive for years, and massively increasing the value of his own stock. Only James Bond can stop him!

Academy Award: Norman Wanstall, Best Sound Effects

Guns at Batasi

1964. Color.

P: George H Brown, D: John Guillermin, W: Robert Hollis, DOP: Douglas Slocombe, M: John Addison, PD: Maurice Carter

CAST: Richard Attenborough, Flora Robson, Mia Farrow, Jack Hawkins, Cecil Parker.

A British battalion is caught in the midst of an African struggle for independence. A splendid performance from Attenborough as a starch-stiff sergeant.

Circus World

1964. Color.

P: Samuel Bronston, D: Henry Hathaway, W: Ben Hecht, Julian Halvey, James Edward Grant, DOP: Jack Hildyard, M: Dimitri Tiomkin, PD: John F. DeCuir

CAST: John Wayne, Rita Hayworth, Claudia Cardinale, Lloyd Nolan.

The Spain-set story follows runaway aerialist Rita Hayworth who returns to the circus to observe her daughter (Cardinale) rehearsing. There later follows a reunion leading to a mother-and-daughter act in the air. John Wayne holds it all together as a typically Western sharpshooting figure.

Those Magnificent Men in Their Flying Machines, or How I Flew from London to Paris in 25 Hours and 11 Minutes

1965. Color.

P: Stan Margulies, D: Ken Annakin, W: Jack Davies, Ken Annakin, DOP: Christopher Chalis, M: Ron Goodwin, PD: Tom Morahan

CAST: Stuart Whitman, Sarah Miles, James Fox, Gert Frobe, Robert Morley, Eric Sykes.

The pioneering days of aviation circa 1910. A newspaper baron (Morley) promises £10,000 to the winner of a London-to-Paris air race, resulting in a wonderfully weird collection of flying machines and pilots intent on winning the booty.

The Ipcress File

1965. Color.

P: Harry Saltzman, D: Sidney J Furie, W: Bill Canaway, James Doran, DOP: Otto Heller, M: John Barry, PD: Ken Adam

CAST: Michael Caine, Nigel Green, Guy Doleman, Gordon Jackson.

Working-class, Cockney Bond-type spy Harry Palmer is sent to retrieve a missing scientist and ends up being captured and subjected to brainwashing techniques. More gritty than the Bond films, and perhaps more like the real world of spies.

Thunderball

1965. Color.

P: Kevin McClory, D: Terence Young, W: Richard Maibaum, John Hopkins, DOP: Ted Moore, M: John Barry, PD: Ken Adam

CAST: Sean Connery, Adolfo Celi, Claudine Auger, Luciana Paluzzi, Rick Van Nutter, Bernard Lee, Lois Maxwell, Desmond Llewelyn.

SPECTRE issues a $280 million atomic bomb ransom threat and the clock is running. Emilio Largo (Celi) is the brains behind the fiendish plot. Lots of underwater action follows in the most successful entry in the Connery series.

Academy Award: John Stears, Best Visual Effects

The Heroes of Telemark

1965. Color.

P: S. Benjamin Fisz, D: Anthony Mann, W: Ivan Moffat, Ben Barzman, DOP: Robert Krasker, M: Malcolm Arnold, PD: Tony Masters.

CAST: Kirk Douglas, Richard Harris, Ulla Jacobson, Michael Redgrave.

Nazi-occupied Germany in 1942 is the setting for this adventure in which Douglas (a reluctant scientist) and Harris (the leader of the local resistance) must destroy a German heavy water plant in Telemark that is being used in nuclear fission advances which could change the course of the war.

Dr. Who and the Daleks

1965. Color.
P: Milton Subotsky, Max J. Rosenberg, D: Gordon Flemyng, W: Milton Subotsky, DOP: John Wilcox, M: Malcolm Lockyer
CAST: Peter Cushing, Roy Castle, Jennie Linden, Barrie Ingham.
Big-screen version of the classic BBC children's TV series. Three kids and their grandfather accidentally start his time machine and are whisked away to a planet where the Daleks rule.

You Only Live Twice

1967. Color.
P: Harry Saltzman & Albert R. Broccoli, D: Lewis Gilbert, W: Roald Dahl, DOP: Freddie Young, M: John Barry, PD: Ken Adam
CAST: Sean Connery, Donald Pleasence, Tetsuro Tamba, Akiko Wakabayashi, Karin Dor, Mie Hama, Bernard Lee, Desmond Llewelyn, Lois Maxwell.
Ernst Stavro Blofeld, SPECTRE number one, is tucked away inside an extinct Japanese volcano whence he launches his space rocket to hijack American and Russian space missions, hoping to start World War Three in the process.

Casino Royale

1967. Color.
P: Charles K. Feldman, Jerry Bresler, D: John Huston, Ken Hughes, Val Guest, Robert Parrish, Joe McGrath, Richard Talmadge, W: Wolf Mankowitz, John Law, Michael Sayers, DOP: Jack Hildyard, M: Burt Bacharach, PD: Michael Stringer
CAST: David Niven, Peter Sellers, Deborah Kerr, Orson Welles, Ursula Andress, Woody Allen, John Huston, Jacqueline Bisset, Derek Nimmo, George Raft, Peter O'Toole.
Lampooned by the critics, this hodgepodge comedy has no central storyline and exists, it would seem, only to provide a vehicle for countless guest stars. A sensible synopsis would be difficult to offer!

Funeral in Berlin

1967. Color.
P: Charles Kasher, D: Guy Hamilton, W: Evan Jones, DOP: Otto Heller, M: Konrad Elfers, PD: Ken Adam
CAST: Michael Caine, Paul Hubschmid, Oscar Homolka, Guy Doleman.
Harry Palmer goes to Berlin to effect the defection of East German spy

chief Homolka. Lots of twists, turns and cliff hangers in the sequel to *The Ipcress File*.

Chitty Chitty Bang Bang

1967. Color.
P: Albert R Broccoli, D: Ken Hughes, W: Roald Dahl, Ken Hughes, Richard Maibaum, DOP: Christopher Challis, M: Irwin Kostal, PD: Ken Adam
    CAST: Dick Van Dyke, Sally Ann Howes, Lionel Jeffries, Gert Frobe, Benny Hill.
    The filmic version of Ian Fleming's collection of children's adventures featuring the fantasmogorical car is brought to life as a musical.

Carry On Follow That Camel

1967. Color.
P: Peter Rogers, D: Gerald Thomas, W: Talbot Rothwell, DOP: Alan Hume, M: Eric Rogers, PD: Alex Vetchinsky
    CAST: Phil Silvers, Kenneth Williams, Jim Dale, Peter Butterworth, Joan Sims, Bernard Bresslaw.
    Accused of cheating in a cricket match, the disgraced Jim Dale (and his manservant) join the French Foreign Legion under Srgt. Knocker (Silvers) and Commandant LaPiste (Williams). Nastiness is supplied by Bernard Bresslaw, his master being Mustapha Leek. The names say it all.

Dracula Has Risen from the Grave

1968. Color.
P: Aida Young, D: Freddie Francis, W: Anthony Hinds, DOP: Arthur Grant, M: James Bernard
    CAST: Christopher Lee, Rupert Davies, Veronica Carlson, Barry Andrews, Barbara Ewing.
    Dracula once again terrorizes the villages lying beneath Castle Dracula in Transylvania, with more emphasis on sex and less on horror in this encounter.

Carry On Up the Khyber

1968. Color.
P: Peter Rogers, D: Gerald Thomas, W: Talbot Rothwell, DOP: Ernest Stewart, M: Eric Rogers, PD: Alex Vetchinsky
    CAST: Sid James, Kenneth Williams, Joan Sims, Charles Hawtrey, Bernard Bresslaw, Roy Castle.
    Arguably the best in the series. The story is set during the Victorian British occupation of India. The feared Scots Guards (the "Devils In Skirts") are not so

feared when one is discovered to wear underpants by the native Burpers. Much comedy ensues along with many stiff upper lips.

Battle of Britain

1969. Color.

P: Harry Saltzman, S Benjamin Fisz, D: Guy Hamilton, W: James Kennaway, Wilfred Greatorex, DOP: Freddie Young, M: Ron Goodwin, William Walton, PD: Maurice Carter

CAST: Laurence Olivier, Trevor Howard, Ralph Richardson, Michael Caine, Christopher Plummer, Susannah York, Michael Redgrave, Ian McShane, Kenneth More.

A top-notch cast headline the spectacular air adventure which boasts some of the best aerial photography and model work on celluloid. Shortage of pilots, planes, fatigue, differing opinions and the ticking clock all combine in summing up the British position — hopeless. Yet they proved otherwise. "Never in the field of human conflict has so much been owed to so few by so many."— Winston Churchill.

Sexton Blake and the Mummy

1968–1971 TV Series (30 x 30 mins)

CAST: Laurence Payne, Ernest Clark, Meredith Edwards, Roger Foss, Eric Lander, Charles Morgan, Dorothea Phillips, Leonard Sachs.

Carry On Camping

1969. Color

P: Peter Rogers, D: Gerald Thomas, W: Talbot Rothwell, DOP: Ernest Stewart, M: Eric Rogers, PD: Lionel Couch

CAST: Kenneth Williams, Sid James, Barbara Windsor, Joan Sims, Hattie Jacques, Terry Scott, Bernard Bresslaw.

Hoping to break down the defenses of their rather prim and proper girlfriends, Sid and Bernie head off with them on a camping holiday to— they think — a nudist colony. Unfortunately, the camp is not nudist and just as they are about to leave in disgust, along comes a group of girls from the St. Chayste Ladies Seminary, and they change their minds about staying!

On Her Majesty's Secret Service

1969. Color.

P: Harry Saltzman & Albert R. Broccoli, D: Peter Hunt, W: Richard Maibaum, DOP: Michael Reed, Egil Woxholt, Roy Ford, John Jordan, M: John Barry, PD: Syd Cain

CAST: George Lazenby, Diana Rigg, Telly Savalas, Ilse Steppat, Gabriele Ferzetti, Bernard Lee, Lois Maxwell, Desmond Llewelyn.

A new James Bond is introduced to the world: He has tracked down his arch-nemesis Blofeld to a Swiss mountain top hideaway where he is planning a bacterial warfare campaign via beautiful women.

The Most Dangerous Man in the World aka The Chairman

1969. Color.
P: Mort Abrahams, D: J. Lee Thompson, W: Ben Maddow, DOP: John Wilcox, M: Jerry Goldsmith, PD: Peter Mullins
CAST: Gregory Peck, Anne Heywood, Arthur Hill, Conrad Yama, Alan Dobie.

When Nobel Prize–winning scientist Peck is in London, he receives a letter from a former colleague in China saying it would be impossible for him to visit. He had no intention of visiting and so is intrigued. He later visits China and meets Chairman Mao, having had a small radio transmitter implanted to record his conversations. What he doesn't realize is that it is also a small explosive device.

The Beverly Hillbillies

1962–71 TV series (274 x 30 mins)
P: Buddy Atkinson, Herb Brower, Joseph Depew, Paul Henning, Al Simon, Mark Tuttle, D: Joseph Depew, Robert Leeds, Ralph Levy, Guy Scarpitta, Richard Whorf, W: various, DOP: Archie R. Dalzell, Lester Shorr, Harry L. Wolf, M: Paul Henning (theme), PD: Howard Campbell, Walter McKeegan
CAST: Buddy Ebsen, Irene Ryan, Donna Douglas, Max Baer, Jr., Raymond Bailey, Nancy Kulp.

Jed Clampett, a true hillbilly, strikes oil when out shooting for food one day and becomes an instant millionaire. He decides that he and the clan ought to move out to Beverly Hills where all the rich folk live — only they don't change their hillbilly lifestyle or outlook, much to the disdain of the wealthy neighbors.

Carry On Again Doctor

1969. Color.
P: Peter Rogers, D: Gerald Thomas, W: Talbot Rothwell, DOP: Ernest Stewart, M: Eric Rogers, PD: Lionel Couch
CAST: Sid James, Jim Dale, Hattie Jacques, Charles Hawtrey, Joan Sims, Barbara Windsor.

When a young, accident-prone doctor (Dale) is offered the option of either leaving or going to serve a mission on the Beatific Isles, he chooses the latter. There he meets Gladstone Screwer (James), who runs the mission, and who also makes a fantastic anti-fat serum. Dale returns to London to set up a clinic and make his fortune from oversized, wealthy women. A few complications ensue from jealous former colleagues.

UFO

1970 TV series
P: Gerry Anderson, Reg Hill, D: Gerry Anderson, Ron Appleton, Cyril Frankell, David Lane, Alan Perry, Jeremy Summers, David Tomblin, Ken Turner, W: various, DOP: various, M: Barry Gray

CAST: Ed Bishop, Wanda Ventham, George Sewell, Peter Gordeno, Gabrielle Drake, Grant Taylor, Vladek Sheybal.

It is 1980 and the Earth is threatened by an alien race who kidnap, kill and use human body parts. SHADO (Supreme Headquarters Alien Defence Organisation) is formed to defend the Earth and operate from a secret location beneath a film studio.

The Private Life of Sherlock Holmes

1970. Color.
P: Billy Wilder, D: Billy Wilder, W: Billy Wilder, I. A. L. Diamond, DOP: Christopher Challis, M: Miklos Rozsa, PD: Alex Trauner

CAST: Robert Stephens, Colin Blakely, Genevieve Page, Christopher Lee, Clive Revill.

Conan Doyle's sleuth plays camp to avoid an assignment from a Russian ballerina and ends up pursuing the Loch Ness Monster.

Carry On Up the Jungle

1970. Color.
P: Peter Rogers, D: Gerald Thomas, W: Talbot Rothwell, DOP: Ernest Stewart, M: Eric Rogers, PD: Alex Vetchinsky

CAST: Frankie Howerd, Sid James, Charles Hawtrey, Kenneth Connor, Joan Sims, Terry Scott.

A jungle set comedy with Tarzan, cannibals, female tribes in search of men to mate with and mistaken tents ... a typical *Carry On* setting, really. Sid James leads a troop of intrepid explorers through the darkest jungles of Pinewood all in search of something: lost children, exotic birds (of the feathered variety) and adventure.

Countess Dracula

1970. Color.
P: Alexander Paal, D: Peter Sasdy, W: Jeremy Paul, Alexander Paal, Peter Sasdy, Gabriel Ronay, DOP: Ken Talbot, M: Harry Robinson.

CAST: Ingrid Pitt, Nigel Green, Sandor Eles, Maurice Denham, Lesley Anne-Down.

Pitt's Hungarian noblewoman restores her youth by bathing in the blood of young virgins in this entry in the Hammer horror catalogue.

The Firechasers

1970.
P: Julian Wintle, D: Sidney Hayers, W: Phillip Levene
CAST: Keith Barron, Chad Everett, Anjanette Comer.
No other details

Twins of Evil

1971. Color.
P: Harry Fine, Michael Style, D: John Hough, W: Tudor Gates, DOP: Dick Bush, M: Harry Robinson, PD: Roy Stannard
CAST: Peter Cushing, Mary & Madeleine Collinson, Dennis Price, Kathleen Byron.

The identical, attractive Collinson twins encounter their witch-hunting uncle Peter Cushing, who learns one of them has been kissed by an undead Count and is now a vampire — but which twin is it?

Dad's Army

1971. Color.
P: John R. Sloan, D: Norman Cohen, W: Jimmy Perry, David Croft, DOP: Terry Maher, M: Wilfred Burns
CAST: Arthur Lowe, John LeMesurier, Clive Dunn, Ian Lavender, Bill Pertwee, John Laurie, James Beck, Arnold Ridley, Liz Fraser.

The big screen treatment for the long running TV comedy following a troop of "Home Guard" soldiers and their toppling of a group of Nazi paratroopers who hold villagers for ransom in Walmington's church.

Carry On At Your Convenience

1971. Color.
P: Peter Rogers, D: Gerald Thomas, W: Talbot Rothwell, DOP: Ernest Stewart, M: Eric Rogers, PD: Lionel Couch
CAST: Sid James, Kenneth Williams, Charles Hawtrey, Joan Sims, Kenneth Cope.

Originally titled *Round the Bend*, this episode is set in a toilet factory at the height of union power. Strikes are called for the smallest of excuses (such as withdrawing the floor tea trolley in the afternoon) — and the comedy moves between toilet humor and pathos with W.C. Boggs' factory possibly closing.

Diamonds Are Forever

1971. Color.
P: Harry Saltzman & Albert R. Broccoli, D: Guy Hamilton, W: Richard Maibaum, Tom Mankiewicz, DOP: Ted Moore, M: John Barry, DOP: Ken Adam
Cast: Sean Connery, Jill St. John, Charles Gray, Lana Wood, Jimmy Dean, Bernard Lee, Lois Maxwell, Desmond Llewelyn.

Connery returned to the role for the "last" time and clearly enjoyed it. With an increase in diamond smuggling in South Africa, Bond is drafted in to investigate. He discovers Blofeld is behind it, and planning a super-intensified space laser using diamond magnification.

The Magnificent Seven Deadly Sins

1971. Color.
P: Graham Stark, Michael L. Green, Tony Tenser, D: Graham Stark, W: Graham Chapman, Barry Cryer, John Esmonde, Marty Feldman, Dave Freeman, Ray Galton, Bob Larby, Spike Milligan, Alan Simpson, Graham Stark, DOP: Harvey Harrison, M: Roy Budd, PD: Roger King
Cast: Ronnie Barker, Alfie Bass, Sheila Bernette, Ian Carmichael, Harry H. Corbett, Julie Edge, Bruce Forsyth, Ronald Fraser, Roy Hudd, Cheryl Kennedy, Stephen Lewis, Spike Milligan, Joan Sims, June Whitfield, Harry Secombe, Leslie Phillips.

A compendium of seven comedy sketches involving the titular seven sins; from Spike Milligan's mainly silent "Sloth" to Harry H. Corbett's "Lust."

The Persuaders!

1971 TV Series (24 x 60 mins)
P: Robert Baker, D: Roy Ward Baker, Basil Dearden, David Greene, Val Guest, Sidney Hayers, James Hill, Peter Hunt, Gerald Mayer, Peter Medak, Roger Moore, Leslie Norman W: Tony Barwick, Walter Black, Terence Feely, Milton S. Gelman, Val Guest, Donald James, Harry W. Junkin, John Kruse, Terry Nation, Michael Pertwee, David Rolfe, Tony Williamson, Peter Yeldham, DOP: Tony Spratling, M: John Barry, Ken Thorne, PD: Charles Bishop, Harry Pottle
Cast: Roger Moore, Tony Curtis, Laurence Naismith.

Wealthy playboys Lord Brett Sinclair and Danny Wilde are brought together by Judge Fulton to investigate crimes the police can't solve. The chalk-and-cheese duo work well together in exotic locations and with glamorous guest stars.

Carry On Abroad

1972. Color.
P: Peter Rogers, D: Gerald Thomas, W: Talbot Rothwell, DOP: Ernest Stewart, M: Eric Rogers, PD: Lionel Couch

CAST: Kenneth Williams, Hattie Jacques, Sid James, Charles Hawtrey, Bernard Bresslaw, Kenneth Connor, June Whitfield, Jack Douglas, Barbara Windsor.

The gang set off for a bit of holiday sun and fun, but instead end up staying at a half-complete, understaffed hotel which crumbles around them, get thrown into prison and discover some fantastic love potion.

Live and Let Die

1973. Color.
P: Harry Saltzman & Albert R. Broccoli, D: Guy Hamilton, W: Tom Mankiewicz, DOP: Ted Moore, M: George Martin, PD: Syd Cain
CAST: Roger Moore, Yaphet Kotto, Jane Seymour, Clifton James, David Hedison, Bernard Lee, Lois Maxwell.

James Bond MK III stars in a more down-to-earth story, pitted against an international drugs baron-cum-small island dignitary after several British agents were killed. Voodoo, speedboats and super locations ensue.

Sleuth

1973. Color.
P: Morton Gottlieb, D: Joseph L. Mankiewicz, W: Anthony Shaffer, DOP: Oswald Morris, M: John Addison, PD: Ken Adam
CAST: Laurence Olivier, Michael Caine.

The two-hander story provided its stars with possibly their best vehicles in the sophisticated game of cat and mouse.

Theater of Blood

1973. Color.
P: John Kohn, Stanley Mann, D: Douglas Hickox, W: Anthony Greville-Bell, DOP: Wolfgang Suschitsky, M: Michael J. Lewis, PD: Michael Seymour
CAST: Vincent Price, Diana Rigg, Ian Hendry, Harry Andrews, Coral Browne, Jack Hawkins, Michael Hordern, Arthur Lowe, Dennis Price, Diana Dors, Joan Hickson, Robert Morley, Eric Sykes.

A star-packed cast headed by Price, who plays an actor who murders the critics who ridiculed his performances over the years.

March of the Zombies

CAST: Vincent Price
(Other details unknown)

Are You Being Served?

1972–85 TV series (30 mins)
P: Jeremy Lloyd & David Croft, D: David Croft
CAST: Mollie Sugden, John Inman, Trevor Bannister, Frank Thornton, Wendy Richard, Arthur English, Arthur Brough, Nicholas Smith, Harold Bennett, Mike Berry, Alfie Bass.

Long-running comedy series based on the goings-on on the ladies' and men's wear floor of a large London department store, Grace Brothers.

The Tomorrow People

1973–79. TV series.
P: Roger Damon Price, D: Paul Bernard, Darrol Blake, Vic Hughes, Dennis Kirkland, Richard Mervyn, Michael Minus, Roger Damon Price, Leon Thau, Peter Webb, Stan Woodward, Peter Yolland. M: Dudley Simpson
CAST: Nicholas Young, Sammie Winmill, Peter Vaughan-Clarke, Elizabeth Adare, Dean Lawrence, Michael Holloway, Philip Gilbert.

The Tomorrow People are British teenagers who hold special powers: They can communicate with each other using telepathy and can transport themselves through the air (Jaunting) and battle the evil folks of earth and space.

Gawain and the Green Knight

1973. Color.
P: Philip Breen, D: Stephen Weeks, W: Philip Green, Stephen Weeks, DOP: Ian Wilson, M: Ron Goodwin, PD: Anthony Woollard
CAST: Murray Head, Nigel Green, Ciaran Madden, Anthony Sharp, Robert Hardy.

A supernatural knight urges the king's men to kill him by chopping off his head. In return, he is entitled to chop off that person's head should he survive.

The Benny Hill Show

1969–89. TV Series (58 x 60 mins)
P: Keith Beckett, David Bell, Ronald Fouracre, Peter Frazer-Jones, Dennis Kirkland, John Robbins, Mark Stuart D: Keith Beckett, David Bell, Ronald Fouracre, Peter Frazer-Jones, Dennis Kirkland, John Robbins, W: Benny Hill & others, DOP: Ted Adcock, Dick Bayley, Jim Howlett, Peter Lang, Roy Pointer, Ray Sieman, M: Albert Hammond, Benny Hill, Boots Randolph, Piero Umiliani PD: various
CAST: Benny Hill, Henry McGee, Bob Todd, Jackie Wright, Nicholas Parsons, Sue Upton & others.

The Return of the Pink Panther

1974. Color.
P: Blake Edwards, P: Blake Edwards, W: Blake Edwards, Frank Waldman, DOP: Geoffrey Unsworth, M: Henry Mancini

CAST: Peter Sellers, Christopher Plummer, Herbert Lom, Catherine Schell, David Lodge, Graham Stark.

When the Pink Panther diamond is stolen again, there is only one man for the job — Clouseau, the bumbling French detective as played so brilliantly by Sellers. Plummer stars as the infamous Phantom and many comic routines ensue as Clouseau sets his trap.

The Man with the Golden Gun

1974. Color.
P: Harry Saltzman & Albert R. Broccoli, D: Guy Hamilton, W: Richard Maibaum, Tom Mankiewicz, DOP: Ted Moore, Oswald Morris, M: John Barry, PD: Peter Murton

CAST: Roger Moore, Christopher Lee, Britt Ekland, Herve Villechaize, Clifton James, Bernard Lee, Lois Maxwell, Desmond Llewelyn.

Francisco Scaramanga (a.k.a. the man with the golden gun) charges $1 million per assassination and Bond, it seems, is his next target, Meanwhile, the solex agitator — a high-powered solar-to-electrical energy converter — has fallen into Scaramanga's hands. Bond is sent after it and to face his adversary on his private Thai island.

Rollerball

1975. Color.
P: Norman Jewison, D: Norman Jewison, W: William Harrison, DOP: Douglas Slocombe, M: Andre Previn, PD: John Box

CAST: James Caan, John Houseman, Maud Adams, John Beck, Moses Gunn.

It's 2018 and the world has been regrouped politically into six sectors. There are no wars, no poverty, no unrest and no free will. To ventilate human's inborn violence and frustration, violent sports are staged. Caan becomes the undisputed champion of one such sport, rollerball. When ordered to retire for fear of him becoming too popular, he refuses.

Tommy

1975. Color.
P: Robert Stigwood, D: Ken Russell, W: Ken Russell, DOP: Dick Bush, M: Pete Townsend, John Entwhistle, Keith Moon, PD: John Clark

CAST: Ann-Margret, Oliver Reed, Roger Daltrey, Elton John, Eric Clapton, Jack Nicholson, Tina Turner, Robert Powell.

Based on the 1969 album by The Who, the story tells of young Tommy, traumatized when he witnesses the death of his father, killed at the hands of his stepfather Oliver Reed. He grows up in an environment of abuse and "escapes" in his own delusions of grandeur. Cameos include Elton John and Eric Clapton.

Carry On Behind

1975. Color.
P: Peter Rogers, D: Gerald Thomas, W: Dave Freeman, DOP: Ernest Stewart, M: Eric Rogers, PD: Lionel Couch
CAST: Kenneth Williams, Elke Sommer, Windsor Davies, Jack Douglas, Joan Sims, Kenneth Connor.

In an attempt to recreate Camping, this comedy is set on a caravan site which has recently been found to be standing over Roman remains. Williams and Sommer play archaeologists whilst the bawdy characters of Davies and Douglas are in search of a few girls!

Carry On England

1976. Color.
P: Peter Rogers, D: Gerald Thomas, W: David Pursall, Jack Seddon DOP: Ernest Stewart, M: Max Harris, PD: Lionel Couch
CAST: Kenneth Connor, Joan Sims, Windsor Davies, Jack Douglas, Patrick Mower.

The last of the traditional Carry On films is set during WWII in an army gun installation—a mixed-sex installation, and that is really the plot. The two sexes get it together over the barbed wire fence.

It Aint 'Alf Hot Mum

1974–84. TV series (30 mins)
P: David Croft, Jimmy Perry, D: John Kilby, Bob Spiers, W: David Croft, Jimmy Perry
CAST: Michael Bates, Windsor Davies, George Layton, Melvyn Hayes, Don Estelle.

In the hot and steamy jungles of World War II Burma, a group of misfit British servicemen form a concert party to entertain the troops.

Bugsy Malone

1976. Color.
P: Alan Marshall, D: Alan Parker, W: Alan Parker, DOP: Michael Seresin, Peter Biziou, M: Dave Garland, PD: Geoffrey Kirkland
CAST: Scott Baio, Jodie Foster, Florrie Dugger, Paul Murphy.

Set in gangster-dominated 1929 America, a wonderful cast of juveniles play out this musical comedy pastiche brilliantly — with everything from prohibition to splurge guns.

Van Der Valk

1972–77. TV Series (60 minutes)
P: Michael Chapman, Geoffrey Gilbert, Robert Love, Lloyd Shirley, George Taylor, D: Ben Bolt, William Brayne, Douglas Camfield, Tom Clegg, Peter Duguid, Graham Evans, Jim Goddard, Don Leaver, Dennis Vance, Mike Vardy, David Wickes
    CAST: Barry Foster, Susan Travers, Joanna Dunham, Nigel Stock, Michael Latimer, Alan Haines.
    The exploits of Amsterdam-based sleuth Peter Van der Valk.

Gulliver's Travels

1977. Color.
D: Peter Hunt, W: Jonathan Swift (novel)
    CAST: Michael Bates, Meredith Edwards, Julian Glover, Richard Harris, Bessie Love, Catherine Schell.
    Gulliver meets the Lilliputians.

Spike Milligan's Q7 and Q8

1978–79. TV series (30 minutes)
    CAST: Spike Milligan, David Lodge, John Bluthal.
    Zany series based on Milligan's humor and observations. The show ran from 1975 (Q6) to 1980 (Q9).

Superman

1978. Color.
P: Pierre Spengler, D: Richard Donner, W: Mario Puzo, David Newman, Leslie Newman, Robert Benton, DOP: Geoffrey Unsworth, M: John Williams, PD: John Barry
    CAST: Marlon Brando, Gene Hackman, Christopher Reeve, Margot Kidder, Ned Beatty.
    The big screen, big-budget treatment for DC Comics' super-strength hero. As Planet Krypton dies, a young baby is sent into space, heading towards Earth in a crystal flying craft. The baby lands on Earth and is adopted by Glenn Ford and Phyllis Thaxter, who discover him. As he grows, so do his powers, which he uses in the fight against evil.
    Academy Award: Derek Meddings and Roy Field, Best Visual Effects

The Muppet Show

1976–80 TV series (130 x 30 minutes)
P: Jim Henson, D: Jim Henson
    Cast (voices and puppeteers): Jim Henson, Frank Oz, Dave Goelz, Richard Hunt, Jerry Nelson, Steve Whitmire.
    Kermit the Frog and his friends run a variety show with a misfit collection of characters: the Great Gonzo, Fozzie the Bear, Miss Pigg and two old hecklers, Statler and Waldorf. Madcap fun that still entertains.

The Medusa Touch

1978. Color.
P: Anne V. Coates, D: Jack Gold, W: John Briley, DOP: Arthur Ibbetson, M: Michael J. Lewis, PD: Doug Ferris
    A novelist believes he has the power to cause disaster — and he does. Tense psychological thriller in which Burton delivers an engaging performance.

Hawk the Slayer

1980. Color.
P: Harry Robertson, D: Terry Marcel, W: Harry Robertson, Terry Marcel, DOP: Paul Beeson, M: Harry Robertson
    CAST: Jack Palance, John Terry, Bernard Bresslaw, Annette Crosbie, Peter O'Farrell.
    Good and evil brother compete for the possession of a powerful flying sword; lots of swords and sorcery ensue in this medieval set adventure.

Outland

1981. Color.
P: Richard Roth, D: Peter Hyams, W: Peter Hyams, DOP: Stephen Goldblatt, M: Jerry Goldsmith, PD: Phillip Harrison.
    CAST: Sean Connery, Peter Boyle, Frances Sternhagen, Clarke Peters, James B Sikking.
    Dubbed "*High Noon* in outer space," *Outland* is a classic good vs. bad story but set on a volcanic moon of Jupiter in the future. Workers at a mining colony are slowly going crazy and Connery's recently arrived Marshall discovers it is due to an amphetamine they are taking. The general manager (Boyle) is intent on increasing the miners' production output by using the drug.

Superman II

1981. Color.
P: Pierre Spengler, D: Richard Lester, W: Mario Puzo, David Newman, Leslie

Newman, DOP: Geoffrey Unsworth, M: Ken Thorne, PD: John Barry, Peter Murton

CAST: Christopher Reeve, Gene Hackman, Terence Stamp, Margot Kidder, Ned Beatty.

Sequel to *Superman* with much the same plot line and cast.

Victor/Victoria

1982. Color.

P: Blake Edwards, D: Blake Edwards, W: Blake Edwards, DOP: Dick Bush, M: Henry Mancini, PD: Roger Maus

CAST: Julie Andrews, James Garner, Robert Preston, John Rhys-Davies, Graham Stark.

Paris, 1934. A girl singer poses as a female impersonator and achieves great success—but complications come with her sex life.

Superman III

1983. Color.

P: Pierre Spengler, D: Richard Lester, W: David Newman, Leslie Newman, DOP: Robert Paynter, M: Ken Thorne, PD: Peter Murton

CAST: Christopher Reeve, Richard Pryor, Robert Vaughan, Margot Kidder, Annette O'Toole.

Pryor is a computer programmer hired by Vaughan — a megalomaniac intent on taking over the world's economy — to control weather satellites. Foiled by Superman, they turn their attentions to fabricating Kryptonite.

Santa Claus—The Movie

1982. Color.

P: Ilya Salkind, Pierre Spengler, D: Jeannot Szwarc, W: David Newman, DOP: Arthur Ibbetson, M: Henry Mancini, PD: Anthony Pratt

CAST: David Huddleston, Dudley Moore, John Lithgow, Judy Cornwall.

The traditional values of Christmas are brought into question when Santa's chief elf (Moore) flees to twentieth century New York after making a bad batch of toys. He ends up working with cigar-puffing Lithgow's crooked toy factory.

Little Shop of Horrors

1986. Color.

P: David Geffen, D: Frank Oz, W: Howard Ashman, DOP: Robert Paynter, M: Miles Goodman, PD: Roy Walker

CAST: Rick Moranis, Ellen Greene, Vincent Gardenia, Steve Martin, James Belushi, John Candy.

Based on the 1982 stage musical, which was inspired by Roger Corman's 1960 film of the same name. Moranis' Seymour works in Mushnik's flower shop. One day lightning strikes and his pet plant Audrey II develops an appetite for human flesh.

Highlander

1986. Color.
P: Peter S. Davis, William M. Panzer, D: Russell Mulcahy, W: Gregory Widen, Peter Bellwood, Larry Ferguson, DOP: Gerry Fisher, M: Michael Kamen, PD: Allan Cameron

CAST: Christophe Lambert, Sean Connery, Roxanne Hart, Clancy Brown.

Initially contemporary, and then transferred to sixteenth-century Scotland, the story follows MacLeod (Lambert) and his mentor Ramirez (Connery), who explains that MacLeod is an immortal who cannot have children but must instead fend off other immortals.

Aliens

1986. Color.
P: Gale Anne Hurd, D: James Cameron, W: James Cameron, DOP: Adrian Biddle, M: James Horner, PD: Peter Lamont

CAST: Sigourney Weaver, Carrie Henn, Michael Biehn, Paul Reiser.

The follow-up to Ridley Scott's 1979 *Alien* is set 57 years later when Ripley (Weaver) comes out of hibernation and heads back to the planet to investigate the loss of contact. After landing, the investigating crew are picked off. It is left to Ripley to, again, face the monster on her own.

The Stone Tapes

1972. Color.
P: Innes Lloyd, D: Peter Sasdy, W: Nigel Kneale

CAST: Michael Bryant, Jane Asher and Iain Cuthbertson.

A scientific ghost story pitting rational investigators against supernatural forces. It inspired films such as *Poltergeist* (1982) and *The Haunting* (1963).

Bert also worked on some 20 or 30 television commercials.

Index

*Numbers in **bold** are page references to illustrations.*